What Readers are saying:

"Jenna Brack's *Pass-Through Place* is an essay collection that is best read slowly. Her light touch with words and her clean writing mirrors the unassuming plains and the openness of sky. But like the subtle beauty of Kansas, there's a depth to this work that settles in with the reader long after the back cover is closed."

—Cheryl Unruh, author of *Gravedigger's Daughter: Vignettes from a Small Kansas Town*

"Reading Jenna Brack's *Pass-Through Place* left me feeling like I'd just taken a long drive with the windows down on a warm summer evening. Brack weaves stories of family, daily life, and personal loss with details about the varied landscape and weather of her home state of Kansas, a place known for its big sky and amber waves of grain. As I criss-crossed the state with Brack through this collection of poignant personal essays, I felt not only the haunting of her growing up places, but a reminiscence that pointed me back to my own. The book is called *Pass-Through Place*, but it's really an invitation to stop and linger a while, both in Brack's memories, reflections, and observations, as well as our own."

—Charity Singleton Craig, author of *The Art of the Essay*

"Woven from her love of place and moments in her lifetime—both unassuming and notable—writer Jenna Brack invites us to pay tender attention to our life at hand, and to the softly worn discovery that 'a place like Kansas rewards the quiet search.' Like a friend sitting with us at our kitchen table, Jenna's writing lovingly invites us to see wherever we are with great care. A heartbreaking, sentient, deeply moving collection of essays."

—Amy Messenger, songwriter and poet

"Jenna's writing is evocative and full of hope as she takes us on a tour of her Kansas—a state that, after reading *Pass-Through Place*, readers will want to do more than just pass through. In each chapter, Jenna takes us on a quest to find what it means to inhabit a place, and what it means for a place to inhabit you."

—Callie R. Feyen, author of *The Teacher Diaries*, *Twirl*, and *When We Swung From Church Bells*

"Jenna Brack's exquisite writing focuses on the diffuse beauty of the Kansas landscape and people through her essays centered on rural, south-central Kansas. Each one unfurls a new corner of her story that unlocks a part of my own experience growing up in the Midwest. As she drives and pines for the glory of a Kansas sunset, I become her befriended passenger eagerly listening and taking in the beauty of this 'pass-through place' in her vivid descriptions of its vastness and through her vulnerable personal narratives. Her writing holds the door open between her past and present, inviting us to linger in the middle space of each story with its richness of color, emotional depth, and tenderness."

—Leslie Iwai, visual artist and creator of *Cumulate*, a permanent installation at the University of Nebraska at Kearney

"If every story of home sounds familiar notes of longing and loss, nostalgia and grief, Jenna Brack's *Pass-Through Place* achieves what the best of home stories can. It evokes a particular landscape while narrating the universal human experience. In *Pass-Through Place*, I follow Brack under the wide, haunting expanse of the Kansas sky; I trail behind through golden fields of winter wheat. Somehow, in these places to which I am a stranger, I yet find myself. Though I pass through Brack's words, they linger with me, as Kansas has lingered with her, lyrically calling me to the rigorous practice of attention. Brack's meditative stories, richly textured in landscape and memory, reclaim the redemptive possibilities of noticing our own lives and land and sky. We can only wonder what else might heal with such a lingering, loving gaze."

—Jen Pollock Michel, author of *A Habit Called Faith* and *In Good Time*

" 'A blank piece of paper can help you see the sky.' In *Pass-Through Place*, Jenna Brack shows us the Kansas sky—grander than the horizon, grander than her hopes. She writes about loving the place you're from, which means loving your weather, your memories, your family, and all the parts of yourself, in all your particularities. Brack's grandmother advises her to look out the window, to pay attention, and to keep writing. Within these pages, we travel the curving roads of life and love . . . all the way home.
P.S. Don't miss the poems!"

—Megan Willome, author of *The Joy of Poetry* and *Love & other Mysteries*

PASS-THROUGH PLACE

Essays on home, hope, and following the horizon

PASS-THROUGH PLACE

Essays on home, hope, and following the horizon

Jenna Brack

Meadowlark Press, LLC
PO Box 333, Emporia, KS 66801
Meadowlarkbookstore.com

Pass-Through Place

Jennabrack.com

Cover Image by Sally Linville
Cover design by Lindsey Bartlett, Meadowlark Press, with Jenna Brack
Interior Design by Lindsey Bartlett, Meadowlark Press

This is a work of nonfiction.

Note: These essays are based on the author's recollections of events and experiences. Events are presented as faithfully as possible but may be subject to the fallibility of memory and the passage of time. In a few cases, names and identifying details have been changed to protect the privacy of individuals, and some details have been compressed for narrative purposes.

Resale and Bulk Orders: Contact info@meadowlark-books.com
https://www.meadowlarkbookstore.com/resale-and-bulk-orders

LITERARY COLLECTION/ Essays
BIOGRAPHY & AUTOBIOGRAPHY/ Women
TRAVEL / United States / Midwest / West North Central (IA, KS, MN, MO, ND, NE, SD)

Library of Congress Control Number: 2025951248

Paperback: 978-1-956578-91-1
Ebook: 978-1-956578-92-8
Audio: 978-1-956578-93-5

For my grandmothers

"I would never have thought this place could be beautiful.
I'm glad to know that."
Father of Reverend John Ames from a graveyard in Kansas
—Marilynne Robinson, *Gilead*

". . . we who lift our voices and pass through, pass through."
—Francis Spufford, *Light Perpetual*

Table of Contents

Pass-Through Place: An Introduction

I am driving across Interstate 70 in eastern Kansas between Manhattan and Topeka on a stretch of road that winds through the Flint Hills. People who call Kansas flat are only partly right—here, in one of the largest tallgrass prairie ecosystems of North America, I am surrounded by low hills dotted with cattle and limestone. The roads rise and fall, the late afternoon sun draping shadowy lines across the valleys.

My two children, ages four and six, are buckled into their booster seats directly behind me, dropping French fries and discarded boxes of chicken nugget crumbs onto the minivan floor. The three of us have recently passed a large wooden sign announcing the Konza Prairie, arguably one of my favorite places in the world with its uninterrupted tallgrass and winding ledges of limestone and shale. I remember fondly the years I spent living in this area during college and graduate school, alternating between studying at the library and wandering prairie trails. Today, as we cruise past, I notice the "K" on the word "Kansas" has tilted sideways. The letter just hangs there, like a set of keys discarded on a nail.

En route to our house near downtown Kansas City, where the view is less prairie and more three-story houses lined with a disheveled trail of construction cones, we have reached the point in the drive where my kids keep asking if we are home yet, and I find myself saying, "Just look out the window—see how those hills are flattened on top?" Or, "Look at the sky. What does that cloud look like to you?" They keep responding that they don't know, and when can they watch a show?

My parenting doubts start rolling in, like these clouds casting shadows over prairie hills. I cannot seem to convince my own children to see the beauty of this place, an area that has shaped so much of my life and imagination. Am I rotting their attention with too much screen time?

Then, a discarded memory from childhood: I have just finished eighth grade, and I am navigating the strange summer between middle school and high school, riding in a conversion van with my mom and grandparents from central Kansas to Washington, DC. There, as part of a history competition, a classmate and I will tell the story of flight—how two founders of a local airline industry built a history of flying. We will describe how Kansas became the Air Capital of the World, a part of the modern story of how people travel from here to there.

But to get to DC, we must drive, for two long days, through what feels like an endless stretch of trees and curving roads. There are so many trees, I keep thinking. You can't see anything through all these trees. I am used to highway drives where I can see for miles, where the flat earth always seems to be racing toward the edge of the sky.

The adults in the car do not seem to feel the same way. My maternal grandma, my Nana, keeps pausing her conversations with the adults up front, then calling to me in the back seat.

"Look out the window! You're missing the view!"

Nana says this over and over again, her "s" sounds whistling through her teeth. I politely ignore her, shoving my Walkman earbuds further into my head, draping my lanky teenage legs across the bench seat, trying to catch some sleep.

But Nana is persistent. She wakes me up from multiple naps, interrupts my Walkman-listening, urges me to look at whatever we are passing. (More trees, it seems.) This feels like a crime—interrupting a sleeping teenager. Don't grown-ups have anything better to do than watch the scenery?

When we finally arrive in Washington, DC, I emerge from the back seat to find myself standing inside the Lincoln Memorial. My teenage detachment dissolves as I experience a place I have only ever seen on television and studied in school. As we stand with our backs turned toward the entrance columns, marveling at the size of the sculpted Abraham Lincoln, we begin chatting with another tourist, a man wearing a t-shirt, hat, and fanny pack (or maybe that's just what my memory wants him to be wearing, because this is the mid-nineties). He politely asks where we are from.

"We're from Kansas," we say, in the no-nonsense way we always talk about our state.

"Oh, yes," he responds, as though he knows the place just as well as the local pub down the street. "*The Wizard of Oz*."

I have heard these references my whole life. But something about this moment sticks and becomes a formative memory that will follow me into adulthood. During a launching point in my young life, I realize I am from a place that many people think of largely in caricatures.

Flat.

Boring.

Flyover.

Just a place to get through on the drive to Colorado.

You're not in Kansas anymore.

But in my mid-thirties, driving I-70 with my own kids in the backseat and surrounded on every side by earth and sky, I *am* in Kansas. Like so many, I have a conflicted relationship with the place where I grew up: even as I wished to leave—and have left—its orbit, I am reminded that even as I journey onward, I must remember where I began.

After living in Kansas for nearly my first three decades, I moved one mile across the state line into Kansas City, Missouri, and began pining for an open view of the sky. Since then, I have journeyed much farther and lived in Europe, land of medieval castles and sidewalk cafés, where physical distance from my home state has sometimes brought echoes of that DC stranger's words: I am from a place seen as small and insignificant.

But in my mind, Kansas is far from small; its landscape looms around the edges of my story, colossal as the sky itself. This is a landscape that seems to have taken up residence in my imagination and shaped my sense of being, becoming for me a sort of "spiritual geography," as Kathleen Norris writes of her experience in *Dakota.* Because I married a man who is also from the area, we find that even as we travel elsewhere, all roads home lead back to Kansas. Through many seasons, I return in an ongoing pilgrimage.

As I have driven Kansas roads and pondered the state's landscape, the region has taken on meaning to me as a metaphor: I understand, intuitively, what it means to have lived in a place so many others will only ever pass through. I know what it means to call that pass-through place home.

In a real sense, we are all passing through, trying to make sense of our lives in this home-but-not-always-home world. Yet we spend many of our days careening through our lives at the increasing speed of technology, struggling to stay awake to the ordinary moments passing around us. What does it mean to pay attention to what is outside our windows? As we journey through our lives and landscapes, what beauty and meaning do we find? Might our own pass-through places also offer a home?

This collection of personal essays describes my life as lived on the Kansas landscape. Many of these stories take place on a physical road or path, then move toward the inner landscape. Often, they move fluidly between time and place, between childhood and adulthood, or into other geographical locations. But at the center of each essay is Kansas, both as a place and a people. Taken together, these stories collectively unfold as a gentle memoir, illuminating how I have been shaped by this setting.

The book is also an exploration of what it means to inhabit middle spaces, to pay attention to ordinary yet sacred moments in our midst. No matter where we are from, these essays are for all of us who find ourselves journeying on long stretches of highway, where there is nothing to see but brown, fallow fields. They are written for those of us who grapple with our hopes under an open sky, one that sends terrifying tornadoes as quickly as the clouds can part. They speak to those who once saw horizons full of possibility but have long ago stopped looking, merely attending to what is directly ahead. These essays are also a lament over the places we call home, and the way they are embedded with not only beauty, but also pain and loss.

My kids are still pleading to watch a show, so I finally pull over to the side of the road and start a movie for them. As they settle into their distractions, the driver's seat admittedly grows quieter, and I focus on the road ahead.

Through the bug-stained windshield, I see I am headed toward two halves of a hill, one that has been cut directly down the middle by the interstate, sliced through its center like a filet. The image strikes me as a symbol of both loss and beauty, a tangible reminder that the land has been carved away, exposing layers of limestone beneath.

As I approach the hill, I begin to experience something that has happened to me many times on these Kansas roads: I perceive I am entering a sort of thin space, where my senses are heightened, time slows, and I am increasingly aware of the details around me.

I glance down at my hands, loosely wrapped around both sides of the steering wheel. I am holding my own directional ticket—a means of going anywhere, at least anywhere I can get to on this current tank of gas. So why do I find myself always returning to this landscape, even as my own years slowly carve away?

I will continue to journey other places, but in this middle place between sky and earth—this horizon space where I am both nowhere and everywhere, never fully staying or fully leaving—I find something calling to me, worth my attention and exploration.

Holding the steering wheel steady, I drive straight ahead. Passing through the middle of the hill, I feel myself headed home.

The Land Grieves

A land acknowledgment

Long before I lived in Kansas, before there were state boundaries or my great-great-grandfather bought farmland twenty miles from where I grew up, the land of my childhood was cared for by many Indigenous peoples, including the Kanza, a Siouan people who would eventually become the state's namesake—People of the South Wind.

In elementary school, I would learn I was living on Native land, though I had little understanding of what that meant. Many years later, while working on a scholarly project during graduate school, I realized anew how costly settler ideals had been for the Indigenous people who first called the Great Plains home.

Even now, the state's expansive wheatfields and gentle rolling hills seem to inhabit a subtle sadness. When I drive them, I often imagine them without roads at all, remembering those who inhabited these areas freely, taking care of the land and its creatures before the presence of Euro-American settlers, my own ancestors.

As I share my stories, I wish to acknowledge those who loved, lived on, and cared for this place before my life began. I mourn the injustices they suffered and honor their contribution. I remember that the land grieves.

The Land Grieves

We learned to sing about amber waves
crowned with grace and triumphant brotherhood.
We acted our way across classroom prairies,
manifested our destiny wearing fake bonnets
in pixelated games of Oregon Trail.
But we never dropped our tears into the ground
for something other than our skinned knees.
No one told us the soil already held so much blood,
No one taught us how to grieve with a land
that already grieves.

—Jenna Brack

Planted

On early roots

"Mine was a Midwest home—you can keep your world."
—William Stafford, "One Home"

When people ask me where I'm from, I usually say central Kansas, and if they are curious, and sometimes they are, they might ask exactly where. Many times, I hold up my left hand and tilt it sideways, so that my palm is facing out. I stretch my palm as flat as I can, though it is not quite flat. My palmar flexion creases run across my hand like narrow rivers, my bones form gentle valleys, the lines and crevices and wrinkles time has written into my skin create texture marking this palm as only my own. I press all my fingers together into small hills, so that the only thing showing is the back loop of my wedding ring around my ring finger.

"Imagine," I say, "this is Kansas, and the little bite from the Missouri River is here in the corner, where my fingers come together. And over here" —I gesture to where my palm stretches wide— "that's western Kansas." Then, I point to a spot just left of my wedding band, not quite in the middle, but almost.

"I'm from right here," I say. "South central Kansas."

Usually people nod in understanding and move to more interesting topics of conversation. Sometimes, they ask more questions, like whether I grew up on a farm (the answer is no), or if I know someone they know who lives there. Or, they might tell their own stories from visiting Kansas, usually from a time when they were trying to get to the Rocky Mountains and feared the flat, open earth of western Kansas would never end, or they share a harrowing tale about being stranded by a blizzard on the interstate and booking a small-town hotel room at the last minute. Often, they remark that they could never live there or make a reference to its obscurity.

Once, in a restaurant overseas, I met an American woman who began recounting her story. Her family had lived in Hutchinson, Kansas, she said, but they moved away before she was born. Naturally, I couldn't keep myself from responding—hearing the name of my hometown all these miles away.

"That's my hometown!" I said.

The woman turned toward me with surprise written across her forehead. "Well then, you know," she said—and here, she casually waved her own palm to the side as though brushing something away—"it's like the middle of nothing."

I nodded. I do know. I know the middle of nothing like the palm of my own hand, all those crevices and valleys and gentle hills and lines. I know wheatfields and endless open sky and steamy summers full of mosquitoes, and I know white grain elevators and tightly wrapped hay bales dotting the side of highways. I know roads that exist in a grid pattern, and I know learning to drive on those roads, and I know real people who live there, like my parents and beloved grandmas and a gaggle of aunts, uncles, and cousins. I know the school where I spent my formative years and the local coffee shop that stocks my favorite chai tea. I know the feeling of being from a place where many people would prefer not to be, and I also know the paradox of not always wanting to be there myself—even having moved far away, yet returning across the years. I know what it feels like to be surrounded by a panoramic sky with the horizon in every direction and watch a sunset slide all the way into darkness.

But I didn't say any of that. Instead, I poked at some creamy green olives sitting on the table in front of me and wondered how my own beginnings had managed to find me, even an ocean away. Perhaps we can never quite escape the places, or the stories, tucked inside the folds of our hands.

In many places in North America, autumn is harvest season, a time of year made for collecting the fruit of one's labor. But for Kansas wheat farmers who grow Turkey Red hard winter wheat, a common variety of Kansas wheat that began thriving after its introduction by Volga German Mennonites from Russia in the 1870s, fall is planting season.

Winter wheat derives its name from the time of year in which it grows—the season when, on the surface, it seems to be doing nothing at all. The wheat, grown in patchwork squares along the outskirts of my hometown and across the state, needs all four seasons of the Kansas climate. After being buried in the earth during autumn, the wheat sprouts, ever so slightly, before it is covered with the cold frost and snow of winter, which insulates the young plants growing underground. Eventually, in the warmth of spring, green stems shoot up and slowly give way to gold in the ripeness of the summer sun, hopefully with heads full of bounty. Then, the wheat that has been planted and tended will become bushels of grain.

But fall is when the planting cycle begins. Perhaps one could say those seeds of wheat are most alive just after they are placed in the ground, buried deeply in the soil, given the chance to grow roots in the quietness of the cold earth. In many ways, fall is a season of loss, as the reds, yellows, and browns of the landscape replace lively green. But just as trees are surrendering their leaves and the natural world begins to fall asleep, the winter wheat begins to live.

I left the hospital one morning in autumn as a premature, jaundiced baby, tucked inside a white gown with lace. I rode on my mother's lap in a wheelchair across the mustard-yellow, low-pile hospital carpet, then through the sliding door onto the sidewalk, until we rolled up to the door of my dad's long, boat-like white car.

In a Polaroid photo from that day, my mom looks so lovely that I marvel how she must have carefully stepped out of bed that morning in her post-labor, nursing-a-baby-all-night state, and managed to curl her hair and apply make-up for the occasion. In the photo she wears a blue jumper with a collared shirt and white bow, her dark hair curled and framed around her face. My dad poses next to her, wearing a matching business suit (an actual suit!). Thirty years later, my husband and I would leave a larger city hospital in our shorts and t-shirts, my hair in a frazzled ponytail, both of us looking completely overwhelmed by the roles we had just been given.

But if my parents were feeling overwhelmed by the birth of their first daughter, they showed no signs, dressed like professionals with me wrapped inside a blanket. Maybe my dad anxiously opened the door or carefully snapped my tiny body into the seat. Maybe somebody from the hospital checked to make sure the seat was installed properly—they were new parents after all.

Then, with my newborn hands curling open and shut, asleep or awake, I do not know, we must have left the parking lot of the hospital and started the eight-minute drive toward the house where I would be raised.

My ride into the world had begun.

Today, I know that drive nearly as well as the tiny spots that dapple my legs on summer days. I would live the next eighteen years in Hutchinson, a mid-sized town in the center of Kansas, a 40,000-person county seat that had absolutely everything you needed and just less than you wanted, an outpost for the surrounding rural area with the larger city of Wichita about an hour away. The city is neither truly urban nor truly rural; even official attempts to define it seem to disagree. "Micropolitan," several sources say, although I am not sure whether the emphasis lies on "micro" or "politan," the latter from the Greek *polis*, meaning city or hilltop.

The ancient Greeks probably imagined anything "politan" as having a temple set on a rocky outcrop, but my hometown was no city on a hill. Most of our landscape, far from the hills of Athens, was that of the ocean-carved plains, a city built on mineral salt deposits with roads as flat as butcher paper, rolled out into a right-angled grid.

Years later, on trips to the hospital where I was born or the nearby doctor's office, my younger brother and I would always ask my mom to drive over a little bump on Twenty-Third Avenue, because to us it felt like a roller coaster.

"Drive faster, mom!" we cheered from the back seat as she sped up the car and took that little bump like a speed racer. A sure sign you live in central Kansas is that a five-foot hill can turn into an event.

Many memories would be made on those roads. But I could never have known on that first ride, as we drove thirty miles per hour down flat, two-lane roads and stopped at a half dozen streetlights, as we passed the Kwik Shop, the local Dillons, the Alco at the corner of Plum and Thirtieth Avenue, that this place would line the edges of my entire childhood.

None of us gets to decide where we are born or where we grow up, even though those places—the staying of them, the changing of them, the good and terrible of them—shape so much of our story. For years, we ride around as passengers in our own lives, going to places before and beyond our memories. Our early setting influences the texture of our lives, our fears and wounds, our beliefs and imagination. Yet we didn't choose these places for ourselves. We inherit long stories, lines of ancestry often as opaque as names listed on a sheet of paper or hung along a family tree, or, if we're lucky, preserved in dusty photographs containing strange faces who share our DNA.

After my own photograph was taken that day, I was driven to a low-roofed, light beige ranch house in the middle of a quiet, unassuming block—a house my parents bought as a foreclosure just before I was born. Today I know that house as if it were my childhood itself—the three concrete steps of the front porch leading to the sitting room inside the door, once a porch until my dad and grandpa turned it into a part of the house. Behind that, a tiny kitchen with a flooring of wood parquet squares, where my brother and I would later play while my mom cooked dinner and tried to step over us. To the left, a narrow family room where we would gather around a small, boxy TV set to watch our morning cartoons on a white-and-blue bean bag, eventually busted from years of use. And near the dining room table, draped in a plastic cloth often smeared with the residue of my mom's wet dishrag and our jellied fingers, was a sliding glass door where, as a jaundiced baby, I was placed in the sun to ease the yellow color from my skin.

Down the hall was a square room with lime-green shag carpet: the little room I called my own. Except for a few early months, I would sleep over the same square feet of ground, in the corner of that small bedroom in the southwest corner of the house, until the day I left for college. Light slanted through dark brown blinds across a crib that would give way to a bed, and toys which would give way to a hodgepodge collection of books, papers, and photos, its contents shifting and growing over days and years. Because I stayed in that place for my most formative years, there would always be pieces of me from every phase of life somewhere in that space, a little of the old always tagging around with the new. And just as the yellow slowly retreated from my premature newborn body, the color, shape, and texture of my early memories would come into existence foggily, like the image of a Polaroid picture slowly emerging, a picture taken long before I was aware the camera lens had snapped.

Like the winter wheat, I was planted—sprouted on lime-green shag carpet with a view of the recently-planted tree in the front yard whose leaves and limbs would grow alongside me. As Christie Purifoy writes in *Roots and Sky*, "The whole planet is ours, but the whole planet is not our home. Instead, home is the ground we measure with our own two feet. And home is the place that measures us."

This place would indeed measure me, sometimes in actual inches marked on a poster-sized ruler behind the door. But it would mark me in other ways too, both as invisibly and real as the map of Kansas across my palm. This place would write its stories into me, influence the stories I would tell and write, and become a setting for my coming and going. What some consider "the middle of nothing" was for me, for a very long time, simply home.

Space, in Four Parts

On young lessons in possibility

"'Dreams take up a lot of space?'
'All you'll give them.'"
—William Least Heat-Moon, *Blue Highways*

I.

In a burnt-orange and cream conversion van, my family of origin cruises across K-96 highway between Hutchinson and Wichita. We pass flattened fields dotted with single silos and small grain elevators, the ground seemingly barren in its cold-weather season, but the sky broad around us. Along this stretch of road, a distance of about forty miles, sprawls the thick web of our family tree—the small town where my dad was born, the family farm where my grandpa was raised alongside his four siblings, and the route toward the small city where my mom was raised. Holidays, birthdays, outings to visit cousins, and learning to drive—many childhood trips lead down K-96.

"Zip!" my mom shouts from the passenger seat. Although my younger brother, John, and I are probably bickering, she isn't shushing us—she's launching us into a game of counting horses out the window.

"Zip!" she shouts again.

My mom, an elementary teacher, always has some creative way to pass road trips. Often her games involve searching for things out the window: horses, letters, license plates, types of cars. Sitting behind her, I only see the back of her dark, perfectly curled hair, but I know her lips are pressed with vibrant lipstick. My mom is like a goddess to me. She looks grand in everything, including nineties high-waisted jeans, matching pant suits in vibrant purple and pink, or floral dresses with belted waists.

"Zip! Zip! Zip!" John, ever competitive, finds a field of horses and claims them as his own.

"Zip! Jenna, are you playing, too?" my mom looks at me in the rearview mirror.

"Yeah," I say. I am, in fact, staring out the window, but I am not motivated to search for animals. If it didn't make me so carsick, I would be reading a book.

"Bury your horses!" my brother calls out preemptively, knowing we are almost to the curve in the road where we'll be able to spot a cemetery. The person who sees the cemetery first makes everyone else lose their points.

"No fair! You have to see it first!" I shout. Even if I have no points, this bothers my sense of justice.

But we are already rounding the curve, and the cemetery leaps into view. "Buryyerhorses!" he quickly shouts again.

"It's fine. I'm not playing anyway," I huff.

I am less upset about the rules infraction than I let on, but somehow, I have already figured out that creating a little drama gives me space to withdraw. Pouting and slinking down in my seat, I stare out the window across a landscape of open fields lined with tidy tree rows. A light blue sky spreads like butter across the ground, currently dry and brown like toast. Not all of Kansas is as flat as the jokes and travel center t-shirts describe, but this part certainly is. It's the only landscape I've ever known, and I find it soothing. The ground and open space pass my window in near-rhythmic consistency.

Even in my earliest years, I feel pressure to be good and responsible much of the time—the firstborn's curse. But when we drive on Kansas highways, I feel myself unwinding, withdrawing into my own thoughts, writing stories in my mind. I love being able to see for miles, uninhibited. I stare out the window, searching for the spot where the enormity of the sky meets the line of earth, wondering how long it would take me to reach it. Out here, my imagination feels free to wander, unhindered as the prairie grass.

II.

The elementary school gymnasium is full of squiggly rows of smelly socks and high-top shoes, bed head and hair-sprayed curls. We sit on dusty, asbestos tiles in squares of rust and green—the same floor on which we play mat tag during PE or spill our half-pint cartons of milk during lunch. We face a wooden stage at the far end of the room that hosts music recitals, talent shows, or assembly speakers. Overhead, the industrial ceiling is peppered with thrown-and-lodged dodge balls, dust-covered fans, and buzzing lights that rise slowly each morning, creating a faux sunrise of fluorescent lighting.

I do not care much for this gymnasium during actual gym class. I hate climbing ropes to the ceiling or being forced to measure how many inches I can stretch my hands past my toes, but my imagination always wants to be moving. My small mind loves exploring big spaces. So when the gym turns from a place for jumping jacks and becomes a gathering place for ideas, it might as well be the Great Hall.

On this day, we are all gathered to hear an author speak. As an adult, I will not be able to recall the author's name, nor what she wrote, though she is likely not famous. If Kansas is, as some say, a piece of toast with a bite taken out of the corner, I am sitting on a small dab of butter right in the middle—a place most well-known authors would fly over rather than visit. But that piece of toast is home, and I love my spot on the tile, sitting in the same room with someone who writes real books.

The author stands in front of the stage, answering questions from the school librarian. I only remember three small words from that day, but those three words are etched into my childhood memory as clearly as if I had carved them into the tile in front of me. During the question-and-answer time, someone raises their hand.

"What inspires you to write?" they ask.

The author pauses. The fluorescent lights buzz overhead.

"A blank page," she says, decisively.

A blank page. I am only in second grade, but these words resonate, as though a tiny bird inside my chest has spotted a crumb and momentarily flutters toward it. I understand. I have my own deep affection for white computer paper, crisp and empty, with perforated strips of early-nineties printer holes lining each edge. I take delight in slowly peeling off those strips of dots, then setting letters onto the open space of each page: lists, poems, stories, newsletters. Sometimes, I even pluck my fingers across the keys of my grandma's old electric Sears typewriter, a gift for my eighth birthday. Every time I press a letter, the keys make a crisp *stss* sound.

A blank page feels like the line of the horizon—an invitation to unwind and start exploring.

For some reason, my mom is also at the assembly that day. (Perhaps she is the room mom? Maybe she wants to hear the author for herself?) The parents who come to assemblies always sit at the back of the gym, lined up in a modest row of chairs.

I see my mom afterward, in the hallway. She gives me a hug, and before I have said anything about the event, she speaks words my memory will hold just as closely as the author's.

"Hey, you know that thing she said about the blank page?" my mom says. "It made me think of you."

III.

On the intersection of Plum Street and Eleventh Avenue in Hutchinson sits a large NASA and Smithsonian-affiliated space museum called the Cosmosphere, a building filled with a variety of important objects like astronaut suits, moon rocks, lunar modules, and rockets. Because it is only a five-minute drive from my school, trips to the museum are standard fare in elementary school, nearly as common as the Friday lunch tray pairing of chili and cinnamon rolls.

On trips to the Cosmosphere, we wear flight gear and crawl inside a replica of a space shuttle. We learn about constellations and discover how astronauts use the bathroom. In the gift shop, we buy packages of freeze-dried space food and play with futuristic lava lamps. We explore the universe, then return to fractions and dreaded gym class, all on an ordinary Tuesday afternoon.

The highlight of each visit to the Cosmosphere is watching a show in the dome-shaped IMAX theater called the Omnimax. The floor of the dim theater is slanted, so I must lean forward and adjust my balance as I walk inside. A large, blank screen stretches across the rounded ceiling, encircling the audience.

We settle into rows of movie theater seats, squirming and giggling. Soon, a voice comes over the speaker.

"If at any point you feel dizzy," the voice says, "simply look down at the floor or close your eyes, and the sensation should stop."

Then the blank screen sparks to life. And from that little dome-shaped theater in the middle of a flyover state, we fly.

We fly to the surface of the moon, to Mars, and soar into the Milky Way. We spot stars, learn about nebulae, and visit the International Space Station. On other visits, we explore wonders here on earth, flying over oceans (which, at this point in my young life, I have never seen in person) and dive inside them to see coral reefs and massive whales. We visit active volcanoes, travel to Yellowstone to get up close and personal with bears, and soar through the Amazon rainforest.

I know we are not really flying, but the experience is so immersive that I often feel myself spinning and must take the announcer's advice to briefly glance down at my feet or close my eyes. With my eyes closed, I remember where I am—still in Kansas, sitting inside a theater—then I open my eyes, again.

I am back in the sky.

IV.

"Whatever you do, do not look at the sun," my third-grade teacher says.

In my hands, I hold two pieces of white paper. Both sheets are completely blank, but in the middle of one page I have poked a single, tiny dot—a pin prick.

A partial solar eclipse is happening during the school day, and we are headed outside to watch. We don't have any fancy light-blocking glasses, but we have prepared for the occasion by making simple paper reflectors.

I grip my sheets of paper carefully as I follow the line of classmates out of the building, past the tetherball courts, through the gravel beds surrounding the tire swings, and onto the big, grassy soccer field.

"Remember, don't stare at the sun," the teacher warns us again as we settle onto the grass. "Just keep looking at your page."

I hold the sheet with the dot just above the second page. Through it, I can see a little white circle: a tiny reflection of the sun. I perch on the grass with my classmates, talking and laughing, as we wait for the eclipse to begin.

Soon, the air around us grows cooler and slightly darker, as though a cloud is passing overhead.

"Okay, everyone!" the teacher says, shushing us. "It's starting."

I look down at my paper. The white circle of light, once a round circle, slowly becomes a crescent as another circular shadow overtakes it. Within a few minutes, the page holds merely a sliver of light—a signal the moon is now nearly in front of the sun.

I am still sitting on my little square of butter, in the middle of the piece of toast, on a grassy playground field. But in the deepening shadows around me and in the tiny, waning crescent of light on the page, I understand something wonderful is happening in space, far above me. Even if what I see on the paper is merely a dim reflection of that brief dance between the sun and moon, I get to hold a tiny piece of it.

That day, I learn an important truth: a blank piece of paper can help you see the sky.

The Seat Next to Grandpa

On harvest and risk

"The time of harvest and the time of poems is passing."
—Anna Kamieńska, *Astonishments*

June blooms across my arms in droplets of sweat. Summer vacation from elementary school has merely begun, but already mornings are the only time of day to safely venture outside without succumbing to the oppressive heat and humidity. Before the sun rises too far in the sky, my mom heads out to her backyard garden wearing a sleeveless shirt and baseball cap. She picks ripe tomatoes, green beans, and okra, and drops them into an empty bucket. Or, if the day's harvest is small, she tucks them into the hemline of her shirt and carries them inside to wash.

Although I am sometimes coaxed outside to help, I rarely volunteer to assist with gardening chores. I am a child of books, with a general aversion to dirt and heat, so I wiggle my way out of anything dirt-related by burying my nose in a story or escaping to the piano. Since we live in town, I do not have farm chores like other kids I know; this little backyard garden is the closest our family comes to growing food ourselves.

But on June evenings, as we eat spaghetti with a side of fresh okra battered and fried with egg and flour, my dad talks of harvest.

"Looks like they'll cut wheat next week," he says. "The crew might start Tuesday, if the rain holds off."

The wide stretches of farmland just beyond the city limits have been slowly ripening, transforming from brown to green to gold. We live on the periphery of farmland, but farming is woven into the vernacular, news, and rhythms around us: crop reports, weather forecasts, conversations about bushels per acre. As a child, simply by absorbing the world around me, I learn harvest involves many factors: the readiness of the wheat, the outside temperature, the dryness of the ground, the availability of combine crews, custom cutters, or wheat trucks. An untimely thunderstorm or hailstorm—common in springtime—can ruin an entire crop.

My Grandpa Don, born and raised in a farmhouse near Haven, still owns his boyhood property and seeds the land each year. He is not a full-time farmer; he serves as the city maintenance man and is known as a jack-of-all-trades, operating a backyard wood shop called "The Board Barn" where he creates everything from grandfather clocks to wooden toys to two-by-fours for construction projects. He teaches Sunday School lessons at the small Baptist church where he is a charter member, and he sometimes fills in for preachers of area congregations using notes he has taken on scripture passages in his half-uppercase, half-lowercase penmanship. He loves to serve, but he also adores being the center of attention and is notorious for telling the same jokes repeatedly, cackling at himself while everyone else groans or offers an appeasing side grin. He eats bowls of peanut butter and honey mixed together into "grandpa's goop," terrible for his blood sugar but delightful for his grandkids, who are offered spoonfuls of the gooey treat alongside him. He is no perfect man—a complicated human like all of us. But even as a part-time land farmer, Grandpa Don is a farmer in the broadest sense, tending to many things within the small region he has called home for his entire life.

We live inside the ecosystem Grandpa Don has tended, too. So for one week each summer, our family rhythms slowly turn along with his, toward the ripening wheatfields. My dad adjusts his work schedule, my mom loads us into the van and drives us down the road to my grandparents' house, and we move our family dinners from the kitchen table to the fields.

———

In Grandma Jessie's kitchen in Haven, the cousins are tasked with making bologna sandwiches. We dutifully place two pieces of white bread on the countertops, slather them with globs of mayo and a slice of bologna, and peel a square of American cheese from its plastic wrapper. My grandma, mom, and aunt drop the sandwiches into plastic baggies and place them into coolers alongside carrot sticks and grapes, plus bags of chips and bottles of water, and load them up for delivery to the field.

We pile into Grandma Jessie's van and make our way out of Haven, just across K-96 highway. Beyond the limits of town, the world divides into steady portions of land and sky. The land is in its golden season, both in color and bounty; Kansas's number one cash crop is ready. Sections of full-grown wheat bend and rise in the wind's ongoing tides, while the cut sections are peeled down to the ground, carved with heavy lines where the combine has already worked. The machines move their green bodies across the field, eating the wheat and spitting the remains out the back. To me, the process feels like a Pac-Man game in slow motion.

We bump our way through the edge of the field, into the sections where the wheat has been most recently cut. As we tumble out of the van, the freshly-cut stalks scrape jagged edges along our bare calves and ankles, leaving white marks on our summer skin. Steam rises from the wheat along with flies and mosquitoes drawn to the coming feast. While we spread dinner in the back of a truck bed, the farmers sense their meal is ready and slowly make their way toward us.

Dinner will not last long—good harvest weather, like the wheat, is a precious commodity. We grandkids quickly stuff sandwiches in our mouths along with the combine crew, then retreat to the field's edge where a narrow line of stalks have escaped the combine blades. We yank the heads off the wheat, holding them in our palms like tiny, prickly caterpillars, then rub their crinkly bodies between our fingers to disperse wheat kernels. This discovery, unfolding these tiny pieces of grain, is our own version of harvest.

After uncovering the tiny seeds from their soft wrapper, we dump piles of them into our mouths, chewing, chewing, chewing until they congeal into grainy gum. We shout with delight when we have finally made something that remotely seems like gum—an unplanned agricultural lesson in food-making.

Then, if we are lucky and well-behaved, we are welcomed into harvest roles beyond bologna sandwich delivery and invited to ride along with the farmers. I often crawl into the wheat truck alongside my dad, where the cab smells of sweat and dirt. Without air conditioning, we leave the windows open to a swirl of cut wheat flecks and dust. My wavy bangs frizz mercilessly in the humidity.

After a fresh load of harvested grain falls from the combine into the back of the truck, we head into town, delivering a load to the elevator. The shorts I'm wearing don't keep my legs from sticking against the seats as we bump down gravel roads, then across the highway to the Co-op and grain elevator, where the load is weighed and deposited. My dad makes small talk with the workers and receives a slip of paper with numbers I cannot understand, then we immediately head back to the field to make the loop again.

But the most coveted position of harvest is not in the wheat truck—it's in the combine, riding with Grandpa Don. If the combine is at the right point in the field, and if my cousins or brother aren't already in line, I am offered a chance to climb into the cab, slide into the narrow opening next to my grandpa, and sit with him while he drives careful rows through the field. Grandpa Don maneuvers the giant steering wheel, guiding the machine in steady lines across the uncut sections. He yells over the engine's noise to describe what he's doing, and I try to listen, hoping I can ride even longer.

From inside the combine, I feel as though I am floating on a yellow sea. The collective stalks of wheat ripple in the wind's ongoing gusts, while the blades of the header rotate, threshing the stalks as they surrender grain to be gathered in the large bin just behind us. Once gathered, the remaining parts of wheat blow out behind the vehicle in a cloud of golden fog.

"Farming is a crapshoot," my high school history teacher says, during a lecture.

We are sitting in vertical rows of desks with our textbooks open, learning about conflicts and important events in the history of the world—places that feel far away from where we now sit. Perhaps we have been discussing one of many periods in history during which agrarian concerns were central, or maybe we are simply talking about the weather. Regardless, my teacher repeats this phrase often—farming is a crapshoot—weaving it through lectures as he scribbles on the overhead projector and walks between our desks as though passing through a small field.

I am familiar with the risks and factors involved in farming, but this is the first time I have heard harvest described this way. It's also the first time I learn the meaning of crapshoot: a gambling term, an implication that farming is nothing but rolling the dice. A game of chance.

"One Kansas farmer feeds more than 155 people + you!" signs say all along Kansas roads, a project of Kansas Agri-Women, reminding travelers that Kansas is a top producer of wheat in the United States, and those bags of flour and packaged bread on grocery shelves are supplied by real fields, worked by real people. Farming is necessary—essential—to the world's food supply.

But this necessary work requires ongoing, dedicated labor. Harvest season is only a small slice of a farming year. Farmers are often growing more than one crop, planting and harvesting across different seasons. But even if you consider the wheat alone, there is always more happening than during one week of summer. As a child, I was only privy to the cutting, but farming is about many other things; readying soil, maintaining machinery, buying and planting seed, and irrigating the land. It's about warding off bugs and deer and other pests or disease that could harm the crop. It is dealing with government regulations and subsidies, or lack thereof. It is daily hard work in the direction of a future moment, trusting that the fallow-looking fields of January still have much happening beneath the surface—that the farmer has work to do, but so does the seed.

Sometimes I puzzle over the subtext in my history teacher's statement. Is he warning us to stay away from farming? To choose a more stable profession? Or is he simply honoring the farmers who sign on for this gamble? Although the conditions are certainly uncontrollable, farming seems like more than rolling dice.

I am not interested in a life of agriculture myself; by the age of fifteen, I am too busy to help with harvest anymore, and Grandpa Don is aging and beginning to hire others to work the land for him. I am interested in my studies and high school basketball games and friends and music. In my dreams about the future, I imagine leaving this place behind and exploring the big, wide world we are now studying in class.

———

In my mid-thirties, Grandpa Don stands at the seventh-floor window of a Wichita hospital, waving his room service menu like a flag. My uncle is standing in the parking lot below, waving up toward the seventh floor at my grandpa, just as the two men agreed five minutes ago. My grandpa's light yellow hospital gown, spotted with tiny geometric patterns, is held together with two strings, but the gown hangs open beyond his awareness. The family members in the room exchange brief looks and suppress quiet laughs, but none of us has the heart to tell him. What does it matter if an old man stands in the window and displays his underwear? Tomorrow, he will have brain surgery for glioblastoma—brain cancer.

After he drops his menu, I move next to him at the window and look across the Kansas landscape. From above the flat earth, we can see for miles. A contrail cuts a giant slice across the sky, a sign of the constant air traffic flowing in and out of Dwight D. Eisenhower Airport and this larger region that has been so important to worldwide aviation. Oranges and yellows from the setting sun poke through graying clouds in slender, horizontal lines. As we look together, my grandpa begins pointing out water towers and grain elevators he recognizes—a region spread before him that he has driven, known, and tended for over eight decades. Relationships he has built, jokes he has told and re-told, seeds he has planted year after year.

Although I don't know it now, this is one of the last times I will see him alert, making us laugh with his antics. The tumor is already affecting his mind and memory, plus heightening his anxiety. Surgery will help for a short while, but the glioblastoma is aggressive. He will not see the next wheat harvest.

A few months later, just weeks before his funeral, we will celebrate his birthday in the fellowship hall of his small-town church. At one point during the party, I will sit down to his right at a white folding table and eat a piece of cake with him. He will not acknowledge my presence; he will not shout over the combine motor or repeat his standard jokes or point out small towns he knows by heart. I'm not sure he will even be fully aware of my presence. Instead, we simply eat together—him hunched over, shoveling his third piece of cake into his mouth with a plastic fork while I politely ask questions over the murmur of the crowd, finally resolving to eat with him in silence. We chew a blend of eggs, milk, sugar, and flour, the fruit of someone else's labor and harvest, yet somehow also the fruit of Grandpa Don's life, which we are here to honor.

From across the room, a photographer captures us together, heads bent over our cake. In the very last photo I have with him, I am sitting in the seat next to him, as if I am riding as a passenger in the combine, watching golden heads of wheat fall into the combine blades. It's still the coveted spot.

One summer day, several years later, my mom sends me a photo of a poem I wrote as a kid, a discovery from my childhood. The poem is about a wheatfield. It is a young, early effort, but it will not be the last of my wheat poetry. I recall reading another poem I wrote about a wheatfield at Southwestern College in Winfield during high school, apparently less deterred by my agrarian beginnings than I wanted to pretend. Even now, as an adult, these images of wheat and harvest keep surfacing, proving somehow essential.

During the same summer my mom unearths the poem, the Kansas wheat harvest is historically poor due to drought—the worst harvest in six decades. On a visit to central Kansas in June, the combines are beginning to work nearby fields, but the full-grown stalks of wheat are noticeably shorter than usual. The heads of grain rise barely to my knee. I have been following the news from a distance, but I am still surprised to see with my own eyes that the wheat is struggling.

"Some farmers are plowing right over their fields and planting new crops," my father-in-law tells me as we drive down the highway one evening. He once farmed, too; he knows the risks of the job.

I think again of my history teacher's voice. Indeed, "farming is a crapshoot." But if we're getting downright honest with ourselves, isn't all of life? Living and loving always place us in the path of risk, subject to despair or storms or glioblastoma. Life is toil and trouble, but we have still been given some things to tend.

I am still more inclined to books than dirt—no expert in the science of farming. Any real farmer or farm family will tell you that the job is less than romantic, most days. But in my mind, farming will always be one week in summer, loops between the field and town, bologna sandwiches and bags of chips and wheat germ congealing into gum in my mouth. It is the heat, the sweat, the wheat heads falling in rhythm, the wind blowing frizzy bangs across my face. It is sitting next to Grandpa Don in the combine and church and knowing that life is rhythm and risk, beautiful and necessary, a sort of poetry.

Dad's Kansas Tours

On lessons in paying attention

"Almost everything turns out to be interesting
if you pay the right kind of attention to it."
—John Green, *The Anthropocene Reviewed*

I am five or six—maybe a little younger or older—riding in the bucket seat of our minivan with my dad in the driver's seat and my mom just in front of me. We are headed home to Hutchinson after having visited somewhere else—maybe our grandparents' house, maybe Wichita, maybe somewhere across the state line. It doesn't matter where we are coming from; it only matters that we are coming home.

Depending on the time of year and the strength or direction of the wind, the air smells like a cocktail of dirt and cow manure, with a hint of oil or a storm brewing to the east. We arrive in the city from the southeast on Yoder Road, crossing highway 50 and cruising across the flat earth at sixty miles an hour. As we cross the overpass into town, we are welcomed by "the skyscrapers of the plains," as they are known on postcards at Kansas travel stops: a smattering of grain elevators with white, narrow shafts connected to conjoined towers. Those towers hold the seed of future bread or dinner rolls, harvested from Kansas farms and waiting to be delivered to the rest of the world.

One of the elevators extends much more impressively than the others—a showstopper of a grain elevator, with perforated edges that crawl along the flat ground for nearly a half mile. My dad draws our attention to the landmark, addressing everyone in the vehicle as though he is our travel guide.

"That's the world's longest grain elevator under a single headhouse," he says, sharing this established local fact while holding the steering wheel steady.

My younger brother and I gaze out the window to our left, gawking at the massive collection of steel and metal, secretly pleased to have such a special landmark right here in our hometown. I do not yet have access to Google to do a fact check, though a later search will tell me nearby Wichita has a grain elevator that is ever-so-slightly longer.

But no matter what the internet says, my dad's voice remains strongest in my memory. Long after I have moved to cities with towering skylines, just up the interstate or across the ocean, when I arrive home in Hutchinson, I will always think of that grain elevator just as he taught me: the longest in the world.

A large, Rand McNally atlas is the star of our 1990s trip planning. Throughout my growing-up years, the atlas is stored in an antique sideboard in the kitchen atop our pile of printed photographs. Whenever we slide it out of its hiding place, we must be careful not to send stacks of Kodak envelopes full of photos and negatives shuffling to the floor.

Sitting at the end of our creamy-white laminate kitchen countertops before a family trip, my dad spreads the atlas before him and begins flipping through it, licking the edge of his thumb before he turns each of the wide pages. After nearly a lifetime of living in Kansas, he does not really need the map. Still, he studies the Kansas page, marking it up with stars and lines, mapping out routes.

"We could get to the Springs on 70, or we could take the southern route, cross highway 50 through Garden City," he might say, mulling over a plan to head west to Colorado.

Or, while planning to head east, "We could drive up through Emporia, then over to Lake of the Ozarks"—he says this more for the rest of us than for himself—"but I think we'll take highway 54, head through Fort Scott."

Later, as I get older and start driving myself, my dad's detailed knowledge of the state begins to guide me around. He teaches me where to find certain roads or signs, and how to find the fastest routes during road construction or traffic.

"The speed limit slows down here, right past this intersection, so watch it," he says from the passenger seat during one of our many driving lessons.

Or, before I head back to college, "If you wanna avoid the construction to Manhattan, just go up 61 to McPherson, then take 56. It goes through Galva," he says, slightly swinging the word Gal-va.

Once, while telling me a story about something else, a small digression teaches me about a Kansas landmark. "On the way to Great Bend, there's this tree, right in the center of the median," he says, chuckling. "Instead of taking it down to make the road, it was easier to just build around it, let it grow."

My brother and I are older, in our early twenties, returning to Hutchinson from college or our city jobs when my dad says, "You guys have time for a drive? I wanna show you something."

We know how this goes. Either we load up in the car now as willing participants, or Dad will wait until we are all headed somewhere as a family, then take the long way there, showing us whatever he intends for us to see. So we hop in the car, and he drives leisurely around town, pointing out things that have changed while we have been away. He shows us a few prominent places, like new buildings or restaurants, but I notice how many of the landmarks he mentions are seemingly small.

"See, this guy over here, he built a new fence," he says, holding the wheel with one hand and pointing his finger out the passenger window.

Then, as we pass another house, "Ya see that guy's gnomes? He's added at least six of them this year!"

We laugh and roll our eyes from the back seat. "One of Dad's tours," I joke, but I am still listening, still learning about Kansas from my dad.

I am in my late thirties now, around the same age as my dad when he first taught me about the world's longest grain elevator. I have recently moved with my young family overseas to Europe—far from central Kansas.

One afternoon, I am texting with my dad across time zones when he sends a picture he has just taken of the garden in his backyard. He has meticulously kept this garden for many years in the same backyard where I used to play games of tag or backyard Frisbee.

Through text, my dad points out that the irises, my sorority flower, are blooming. Then he adds, "I planted wheat in the middle last fall. Can you spot it?"

I search for a few minutes, but I cannot spot the wheat, so I pass the photo to my seven-year-old daughter. She throws out a few guesses, but we're both stumped. From overseas, we cannot seem to find that iconic Kansas wheat.

"Right behind the hostas plant," my dad nudges, and then I finally spot it—a bundle of green, early stage, sprouting wheat.

I have traveled miles from Kansas, but somehow, my dad is still giving me a tour, always teaching me about the place I grew up and its many landmarks, big and small. From across the ocean, I can see him stretching his hand toward the window to show me something—pointing out everything I missed while I was gone.

Broken Curb

On learning limits

"I needed a story to propel me forward . . ."
—Callie Feyen, *Twirl*

I love the Kansas landscape for its openness—the seeming limitlessness of the ground and sky throughout its rural areas. But most of my young life is lived in town where the landscape is largely residential: asphalt roads with speed limit signs and traffic lights, curving lines of tar sealing over cracks, front yards with shrubs and oak trees, chain-link fences running in tidy lines between each home. If my brother or I kick a ball or throw an errant Frisbee in our backyard, it can sail over any number of fences and end up on a neighboring property.

Usually our runaway toys land in the yard just to the north where a quiet woman grows a thick hedge of roses along the fenceline and fastidiously plucks weeds out of her front yard by hand. Like Scout and Jem deciding who will sneak onto the Radley property, my brother and I bicker until one of us finally surrenders, becoming the sibling who must nervously slink through the gate into the woman's yard without getting caught, before tossing the item back across the rose bushes to safety. Or, if we are feeling less brave and the item seems within reach, we might attempt to stick our hands through the wire fencing and bramble of thorns, carefully sliding it back through without mercilessly scratching up our arms.

These are my early lessons in boundaries. Although my imagination wants to explore, in the real world there are fences and thorns and neighbors who wish you would not keep throwing balls into their yard.

As I grow older, of course, freedom from that house and yard becomes increasingly important, and a ticket to my freedom as I enter adolescence is my driver's license. Aside from two weeks of standard driver's education, I mostly learn to drive from my dad. His exhortations to pay attention extend heartily to our driving lessons.

"Now put the car into drive. Check your mirrors. Now slowly, I said *slowly*, lift your foot off the brake. Do you feel the engine shift? Lower onto the accelerator. Lightly, lightly. Do you see this car over here to your left?"

Hour after hour, one detailed lesson after the next, he turns me into a careful, attentive driver—or so he thinks.

As my sixteenth birthday approaches, I haven't set my hopes high for a car. My parents are reasonable people, and although no one has told me how I will be getting around once my license is official, I assume I will be offered an occasional loan of my dad's car or asked to buy a boat-sized car with a strong engine, or, if I am lucky, granted a boring but reliable car to call my own.

But when my parents lead me into the garage just before I turn sixteen, I discover a surprise: a 1993 Toyota Paseo—a low-to-the-ground, two-door car, painted in shiny teal. The car is used but adorable, with a working CD player, a small sunroof, and a radio antenna that travels up and down with only the push of a button.

When I sit inside that car for the first time—an adolescent introvert's paradise where no one can hear me or contact me (in a glorious age before the ubiquity of cell phones)—I sing my heart out, practicing for an upcoming high school musical.

I feel free.

Two weeks later, reveling in my newfound freedom, I am driving myself to an after-school piano lesson in my Paseo. The lessons are in an older, historic area of town where the roads are made of uneven brick. My tires tumble across the bricks as I drive, the texture of the road lightly jostling me as I roll up to the side of the road to park, still moving too fast.

Thud.

POP.

Scrrrrrrratch.

A cold chill starts in my head and slides down my body. My foot presses the brake, but the rest of me is overtaken by panic, a feeling I have known keenly whenever I fear I have done something wrong, except this is much worse than an errant ball over the fence. As if in slow motion, I shift the car into park. I guide myself to turn off the engine and step out of the car, my shoulders full of nervous energy. I have not started crying yet, but the pattern is predictable: after the panic wears off, the tears will come.

The brick road is lined with concrete curbs in nearly perfect geometric right angles, high and square. I push the driver's side door open and walk around to the passenger's side. As though to spite me, in the very place I have tried to park, the curb is broken. A piece of concrete juts out unevenly, several inches toward the street—and now, into my front tire and passenger door. All along the passenger door, an ugly, deep scratch mars my car, and teal paint decorates the edge of the curb.

Teal paint from my new-to-me car.

For much of my young life, I have been guided by an unspoken philosophy: make no mistakes. Perfectionist. Achiever. Good grades, good behavior, rinse and repeat. These things earn me accolades, but in ways I cannot yet describe or articulate, I slowly begin to wear them like an implicit pressure, a feature of my personality. I suppose this strategy is an attempt to gain some control. Avoid mistakes, and maybe I can minimize the messy chaos of living. But coming of age is about growth—and growth is messy.

I had wrecked one other vehicle before—a golf cart. In the grassy acre of Grandpa Don's backyard, my cousins and I were goofing around, taking turns driving the golf cart when I came around the corner and forgot to brake. I smacked right into the side of my grandpa's woodworking shed, leaving a permanent dent in its red side. I felt that familiar cold chill, my head swirling just above my shoulders.

But after hearing the crash and coming over to check our safety and survey the damage, Grandpa Don had mostly brushed it off. "I'm just glad everyone is okay," he said, though I do remember my golf cart driving privileges ending around then.

Still, the dent in the shed remained. For years, it served as a reminder for my family to tease me about my poor driving, and a reason for me to feel a flash of regret. But over time, that wound on my grandpa's shed also grew into something else—merely a small dent on the larger landscape of my life, a tale we would tell each other and laugh. *Remember the time . . .*

Mrs. Janzen, my piano teacher, lives in a small, white bungalow on Sixteenth Avenue. I have been visiting her home weekly since I was in second grade, showing up and letting myself in the back door, playing puzzles or reading magazines until my turn to rehearse.

Mrs. Janzen is a thin woman with short hair and glasses who writes in loopy cursive letters and creates homemade ornaments for her students each Christmas. She is a kind soul with a tender, measured voice, although like a true musician, she is not a pushover. I've observed most musicians are quite gentle and friendly—until you violate the time signature.

Lessons begin at the black, baby grand piano in Mrs. Janzen's living room, which takes up nearly the entire front room. The other furniture is pressed back against the walls and windows, squeezed into all the remaining spaces. The piano is the focal point; everything else moves aside for the music.

Because these are piano lessons, I watch Mrs. Janzen's hands all the time, admiring the way they move across the keys so fluently and in control. I love those hands because they can make music—rich and full, filling her tiny living room with a sound I, too, want to make. I recall how, in our very first lesson, she taught me how to position my hands on the keys gently, with just a bit of curve.

"Act like a tennis ball is sitting beneath your palms," she said.

In my first recital, I played a song called "The Juggler." The recital was in May, and I had been outside over the weekend, resulting in a terrible sunburn that made my second-grade brain worry I wouldn't be able to move my arms. As if echoing those fears, the song's simple lyrics underscored the difficulty of juggling, with the speaker worrying that tossed objects might fall and break into pieces.

I didn't drop any notes that day. But eight years later, still showing up weekly to this bungalow on Sixteenth Avenue, the anxieties of my first recital song's speaker make much more sense. The years have given way to more complicated notes and more complex songs. Now, my hands hold my fresh-off-the-press driver's license and my worry.

I leave my car on the roadside and slip through Mrs. Janzen's back door, the tears coming now, the confession poised to slide from my lips.

———

Here is the secret no one knows about growing up while it is happening: you grow up, but you also don't. Some parts of you play out across your lifetime like an anthem, maybe hiding for a while but always returning to a similar melody with a slightly different phrasing.

I will fear making mistakes for a long time.

In my late thirties, all grown up with children of my own who practice their own piano lessons, I join a cohort of artists focusing on our mental health. I am making music only for fun these days, but I am still an artist, creating melodies most often through words. But in this creative endeavor, too, I still bump up against many limits.

But that's why this cohort has gathered. We've come together because artmaking is essential and, in a world of capitalist pressures and constant performance metrics, the things we keep bumping into are more jarring than jutted-out curbs. They are critics, fear, and anxiety, and the only way to move forward is to tend to this person inside ourselves. We must learn to treat these younger parts of ourselves with grace and compassion.

A therapist trained in Internal Family Systems leads us through an exercise.

"Scan your body," she says. "Are there any parts calling out to you?"

I immediately sense a knot just beside my shoulder blade on the right side. A lifetime of pressure seems to have lodged itself here.

The therapist invites us to think about what part of us that feeling represents.

Anxiety, I know. I have known it well in my body, but I have never pictured it before, sitting with me. But when the therapist encourages us to imagine this part—akin to character emotions in the movie *Inside Out 2*—she appears, a woman whose arms are wrapped tightly around her chest, tense and nervous, fearful of anyone who tries to get too close.

"How old is this part of you?" the therapist asks.

Some of the questions she asks are hard, but this one is not difficult. Even though I have driven many miles since then, still not the best at parking, admittedly, most of my anxiety is no older than the sixteen-year-old girl who wrecked her car into the curb.

I examine her from the perspective of a much older me. I see her there, on the side of the road with her wrecked car and the pressures of performing. I want that part of me to heal. I want her to transform from a protector into something like a wise, old owl with an ability to withstand some struggle and come out laughing.

I want her to remember that beyond that neighborhood and those brick roads and the broken curb on Sixteenth Avenue, a big panoramic sky and spacious open fields lead all the way to the horizon.

Mrs. Janzen welcomes me inside. By now, I am crying, and I sense her concern. I shakily present my accident report, and she is full of empathy and gentleness—the calmest of first responders. She leads me to a phone attached to the wall with a long, curly cord and waits while I dial my parents' number. I poke my fingers into the rotary dial, finding each number and spinning it to the right, ringing my parents' kitchen on the other side. My mom answers and assures me someone will be there soon, then I wait with Mrs. Janzen until my dad arrives.

I suppose my dad has every right to be angry, seeing as it has taken me only weeks to wreck my car, even after all those lessons and exhortations to pay attention. But to my relief, he is calm, at least outwardly. He surveys the damage and makes some calls and drives me home, and I receive a few more lessons in parking while the car is being fixed. I keep returning to my weekly piano lesson—eventually in my teal car, again—and continue passing that spot on the curb, albeit more carefully this time.

The teal paint remains on the curb for many months. Perhaps it's still there even after I load up the teal Paseo with boxes packed for my dorm room and drive it away to college. But over time, the incident becomes one more tale woven into the lore of our family, yet another mistake that somehow grows into a story.

I Told You So

On siblings and growing up

"'Everyone is a bit scared,' said the horse. 'But we are less scared together.'"
—Charlie Mackesy, *The Boy, the Mole, the Fox and the Horse*

The ice storm started, as Kansas weather often does, with ominous forecasts from meteorologists, followed by repeated calls from my mother to ask if I had been keeping an eye on things, and then, for several unnoteworthy hours where small clouds tiptoed lightly across the Kansas plains, by the appearance that nothing would happen at all.

That morning, I was in the Kansas City area for a job interview. I wore a light blue shirt beneath a creamy brown business suit, which I had purchased just for the occasion. The pant legs were too long, but I had no time to get them hemmed, so I wore tall, closed-toe heels. They seemed appropriate when I tried them on in front of the mirror, but as I discovered a little too late, the heels slipped badly across the tile in the school building, and I had to walk at an awkwardly slow pace to stay on my feet.

Despite my clumsiness, I made it through the interview. With the formal questions behind us, we turned to more pressing matters—the weather.

"They say ice is on the way," the assistant principal said. "Wonder if we'll have school tomorrow."

Just a year later, working as a teacher in that very building, I would have eagerly prayed for any weather that meant a possible day off from school. But this was the end of my senior year in college, and I was headed into finals week. I had already walked the stage at graduation and finished student teaching, and it was my last week to live in a house with seven friends who had become more like family. My storm concerns were focused on only one thing—getting back to Manhattan, Kansas, two hours away.

Only, I didn't have a car.

I had caught a ride to Kansas City, intending to spend another night there before heading home. But as I listened to weather reports that afternoon, in a way that surely would have made my mother proud, I knew this plan would only keep me stuck longer.

"The ice will start around six o'clock," the forecasters kept saying. "This event will be very serious."

I reached out to everyone I knew who might be driving from Kansas City to Manhattan that day, but no one was crazy enough to get on the road with a major storm looming. Just when I had concluded there was no way to make it back, a college friend called.

"My dad is heading home to Lawrence but can take you as far as Topeka," she said, along with instructions on where to meet him at the end of the workday.

Topeka was halfway. Halfway was good enough.

I met my friend's dad at a parking lot near the toll booth on I-70, carrying my business suit on a hanger inside a flimsy plastic bag. After loading my suitcase into the car, we set off to beat the storm. As we drove, we made small talk, each of us suffering through the discomfort of riding with someone we had not expected to share this hour with, yet grateful for company at a time when everyone on the road seemed eager to be home.

Out the passenger window, the weather still looked normal for a December day: gray, cloudy, and cold. I wondered if the meteorologists, bless their efforts, had been wrong. I had lived through many "snow days" based on forecasted reports of three to five inches where we received merely a dusting of snow. Then again, I had also lived in Kansas long enough to know that prairie weather is finicky and can change without warning.

When we arrived at Wanamaker Road in Topeka, I gestured to the parking lot of a Freddy's burger chain. "You can just drop me off," I said, sensing my ride was anxious to get back to Lawrence before the weather worsened, and grateful he had already done me a significant favor by driving farther than he had intended. I waved goodbye and schlepped all my things inside, dismissing stares from other restaurant patrons. Then, after piling into a booth with my suitcase and business suit, I waited on my ride for the next leg of my journey—John, my younger brother.

John, who also went to school in Manhattan, had agreed to drive an hour to pick me up and take me back home—one of many sibling favors I never knew I would need to call in. By this time, it was six o'clock and the storm was slated to start, but he wasn't there yet, so I ordered myself a burger and waited.

My brother is fiercely loyal, both to people and causes. As a teenager, I once witnessed him sit by my parents' bedside for an hour, begging for extra time on his curfew. I'm pretty sure my dad didn't even respond for most of that hour—he just kept flipping channels on the TV, unaffected by the spectacle. But John was determined to negotiate his later time, even if he missed an extra hour of plans on the front end. My brother also gives the world's best bear hugs, which I believe he honed throughout a lifetime of tackling me to the carpet, practicing his "wrestling moves." Still, at the end of the day, those tackles always became hugs—his soft heart stronger than his brotherly bite.

So I wasn't worried about whether John would show up. I knew he would be there. I did worry about what time he might arrive, and how grisly the weather could get before then.

By the time John appeared, the sky was indeed spitting against the windowpanes at Freddy's. "You have everything?" John said, entering the side door of the restaurant along with a burst of cold air. He wrapped me in one of his characteristic hugs and picked up my suitcase, brushing ice crystals off his sleeves.

"How is it out there?" I asked.

"It's coming down, but we'll be okay," he said, leading me back out to his pale brown Camry. We loaded into his car, then began our slow journey down Wanamaker Road, onto the exit ramp, and up onto the lonely stretch of interstate between us and Manhattan.

In good weather, I-70 between Topeka and Manhattan is one of my favorite sections of interstate. Across those fifty miles, the landscape transitions from the rolling, tree-covered hills of the eastern half of the state into the more open, shale and limestone rock formations of the Flint Hills. But in bad weather, when the Kansas wind is whipping sideways across the lanes, the air whistling in mysterious gusts and gathering force in the spaces between each hill, or when snow is blowing across the road in whitened sheets, the road can be extremely dangerous. The area is largely rural, with very few gas stations or service shops and a hefty amount of semi-truck traffic.

Just a few years earlier, the professor of my fiction writing workshop had walked into class with red, puffy eyes, clearly weeping. Another student, a quiet girl who often sat at the table just across from me, but who I didn't know well, had died on that very stretch of road, when a semi hit her car from behind.

The memory made me shudder as we pulled onto the four-lane highway, the wind already picking up, snow and ice coming down all around us, pinging against the passenger window. If it had been merely spitting ice at the restaurant, then out here, with no city protection, the ice was ricocheting off the windshield. The winter sun had already slipped behind the earth, and the December darkness meant we could see little except a swirl of energetic crystals in my brother's headlights, plus the brake lights of other cars slowing down or pulling over to the side of the road.

I had my seatbelt fastened, but otherwise, I was truly sitting on the edge of my seat. Only a few miles in, we passed cars already in the ditch, and others had pulled over with their blinkers flashing. Semi-trucks crept along beside us.

Despite the elements, my brother drove a little faster than I thought he should. "John, maybe you should slow down?" I said.

"We'll be okay," he assured me again, keeping his eyes on the road. I tried to avoid pressing my foot against imaginary brakes and wondered how my little brother had grown up into the one trying to take care of *me.*

Once, when we were kids, John about five and I seven, our neighbors were playing with a skateboard in their front driveway. We were all enamored with this board on wheels, having never used one before. Each of us took turns sitting our little bottoms on the board and pushing ourselves around the neighbor's driveway with our feet.

But when it was John's turn, he refused to stoop and sit like the rest of us. He just stood right up on top of that skateboard.

I saw the trouble coming instantly and yelled at him in my bossiest older-sister voice.

"Jamark!" We called him John Mark in those days, and I always shortened it into one word. "You better sit down!"

Let this be on record: I warned him.

Only seconds later, as though foretold by his wiser big sister, John hit a bump in the driveway, fell off the skateboard, and smashed into the concrete, squarely onto his front teeth. Blood burst from his mouth and our friends stared wide-eyed as I ran screaming back to our house and through the front door.

"Mahhhhhm! Jamark's hurt!"

As my mom dashed out the door to tend to his injuries—then immediately put him in the car to take him to the dentist where he would receive a fake tooth—I, trying to protect my innocence, told her several times, "Mom, I told him not to stand up. I told him not to stand!"

Now, driving in the blizzard, I wanted to rehearse the moment for him again, to say in my older-sister voice, *remember all the times I told you so?* But driving on the interstate in whiteout conditions was probably not the time. I kept my thoughts to myself.

Of course, this was not the only road trip we had been on together. I remembered many days of sitting in the back seat, drawing imaginary lines with our fingers down the upholstered bench, creating a boundary the other sibling could not cross (but always did). I will never forget one vacation where John was obsessed with the golden arches of a particular fast-food joint and kept announcing their presence each time he spotted them. Later, as high school students, we flew across the ocean on a volunteer trip and slept on each other's shoulders, grateful to have a sibling next to us during a fourteen-hour flight. John had also been there for all those trips down Twenty-Third Avenue to the doctor's office when we asked my mom to drive faster over the little hill and on rides in our family's conversion van to visit our grandparents. He, too, had ridden with my Grandpa Don in his combine and taken many of our dad's tours around town.

But we had been passengers in those moments. Now, we were both finding our own way of driving through and being in the world, navigating college and finals and job interviews and major ice storms. We grew up together on this Kansas landscape—it had surrounded us and been a co-witness to our childhoods. But that same landscape now threatened and pressed in on us. Inside the ice-wrapped car, we became almost childlike again, the two of us passing across a landscape still much bigger than us.

Across those fifty miles, the ice never relented. The storm only grew more ominous, covering the road in tiny white beads and wrapping the car in ice. But minute by slow minute, we kept trudging forward, John trying to distract me with other topics of conversation while I clung to the side of the cloth-covered passenger seat. I don't think I exhaled until John pulled up in front of my rental house where my friends were waiting inside. I thanked him profusely before getting out of the car, and then, he pulled an older-sibling on me.

"See? I told you we'd make it back," he said.

The verdict is still out on whether that dangerous drive was worth it. Not even an hour after I settled onto the couch to watch a show, happily surrounded by my roommates, the power went out. Ice coated and downed power lines all over the city and region, dropping huge tree branches in blockades across the roads. We spent the rest of the week without heat, sleeping inside layers of blankets and talking by candlelight, slip-sliding our cars to local restaurants to charge our phones. Our university campus lost power, too, and finals week was entirely canceled. It was the ice storm of a century. Even now, the National Weather Service has that storm listed as the worst ice storm ever to hit Kansas. Recalling the event, their website reports, "damage to trees, power lines and power poles was obviously staggering and made any attempt at travel treacherous, if not impossible."

Years later, in our thirties, I asked John if he remembered that impossible storm. We hadn't talked much about the drive after it happened, as our young adult lives had quickly tumbled into the concerns of next-semester plans, moving boxes, holiday travel, and all the ordinary crises of growing up into adulthood.

John was eating dinner when I asked, inside a Topeka home where he lived for a short season, not far from the Freddy's on Wanamaker. He immediately paused chewing and looked up. He laughed, but as he did, he leaned his torso across the table and looked at me with the expression of a person who has witnessed the unbelievable. "That was crazy," he said. "My car was encased in ice when I got back." I sensed he had been more nervous that night than he ever let on.

Maybe I could not keep him from busting out his front tooth in a skateboarding accident when we were little, but when the tables were turned and I wanted to do something risky and unnecessary, in a season when I was tiptoeing on the edge of adulthood, afraid I might slip off my heels and get stranded from friends who felt like family, my little brother showed up at a hamburger joint in the middle of a historic storm and drove me through—just like he told me he would.

Tornado Clean-Up

On picking up the pieces

"You couldn't get blown around in a tornado,
he said, and not get banged up."
—Leif Enger, *Peace Like a River*

I steered my white Corolla off the interstate where the signs pointed to Chapman, Kansas. Orange cones and wooden barriers stretched across the road, forcing traffic to stop and check in with a volunteer holding a clipboard. Vans from the Red Cross and other agencies had already arrived on site, while buses and church vans rolled in next to me, carrying groups of volunteers.

"Hi, I'm alone," I told the volunteer when it was my turn to check in. "I'm just here to help." She took my name and ID and, as she looked it over, I worried she might turn me away since I had no official affiliation with any group. I had shown up here unannounced—a recent college graduate wearing jeans and tennis shoes, holding a single pair of work gloves I had borrowed that morning from my dad.

But the volunteer waved her arm past the cones. "Just go that way, and you'll see the volunteer tent," she said, handing me back my ID. I drove on, relieved she didn't refuse a twenty-something woman with skinny arms and a soft heart, which is maybe all a person needs to be useful during tragedy.

Just a few days earlier, an F-3 tornado had torn through a section of east-central Kansas. Gathered around the television in my parents' kitchen where I was spending a few weeks of summer, we watched live reports as the tornado devastated places along its path, including Manhattan, where my brother lived. We exhaled when my brother called to say he was safe, and his rental house had avoided any damage. But the tiny town of Chapman, Kansas, had not been so fortunate.

I had never heard of Chapman before. Perhaps I had seen its name on interstate exits or on maps, but I had no reason to visit there. Yet the tornado took senseless aim at that small town, tearing a path six blocks wide through its center, destroying nearly eighty percent of the businesses, schools, and homes. The state immediately declared an emergency and called for relief aid to help clear the rubble.

I am not usually the type to volunteer for hard manual labor, but I needed to keep myself busy and distracted, so in an effort that was less noble than desperate, I determined to help with the clean-up. I climbed into my Corolla and drove toward the disaster scene.

I suppose it's impossible to emerge from childhood into young adulthood without experiencing heartbreak, much like it's impossible to spend years living in Kansas without witnessing the effects of a tornadic sky. Sometimes the conditions simply billow into grief when you are least expecting it, and you must give way to the inevitable fragility of being human.

In the short months between college graduation and my first teaching assignment, I had gone to Colorado, imagining the steps to my future were laid out neatly before me, like the mountain trails I explored during those weeks. Instead, surrounded by evergreens and layered rock formations, I experienced an unexpected loss—a broken heart.

Before hiking, trail guides teach you to stay vigilant for sudden thunderstorms, especially lightning strikes. But it's rare for tornadoes to form in the rockier terrain and lower atmospheric pressure of the mountains.

Yet this grief sent me spinning, my internal landscape becoming disorienting and unfamiliar. For weeks, I sat on the edges of boulders and stared into the sky, wondering what to do, and where to go, next.

In my despair, I wanted to escape any semblance of my old life—to start over and go somewhere new. But I had already made some commitments, including accepting a teaching job back in Kansas. When I told a mentor I was thinking of breaking the contract and starting my search over, although it was now late in the hiring cycle, he encouraged me otherwise. "Keep the job," he said. "You'll make it through."

I wasn't so sure. But in spite of my resistance, I recommitted to the plan. The job was on the far eastern edge of the state—just about as far east as you can go and still be in Kansas—which meant my pilgrimage that summer involved traveling four hundred miles, down out of the Rocky Mountains, across the wide, level plains of western Kansas, into central Kansas, up through the rolling Flint Hills, and into the Kansas City region until I was only twenty miles from the Missouri state line.

To begin my young adult life, I would first take a journey across the state in which I had grown up.

If you had asked me, in those days, to define adventure, I would have described it as going somewhere grand: Paris, London, New York, or at least a decent-sized city like Chicago. I was not expecting adventures to happen on ordinary days, in ordinary places. I was always looking forward, searching for the next thing, hoping to be swept into something exciting.

After all, doesn't anyone important travel far from home? Think of our great Western literary myths. The Hero's Journey, as described by Joseph Campbell. Even *Finding Nemo*. Most stories involve people going somewhere—yet here I was, headed back. Even though I would live in a part of the state I had never lived in, it still felt like returning when I wanted to be anywhere else.

As I crossed the state line back into western Kansas, the plains stretched before me like a sheet of blank paper. This part of the state is how most people imagine Kansas—completely flat, open earth, with a sky "like a person yawned and never stopped," as Ian Frazier writes in *Great Plains.*

"Be careful," I said to a friend once, who was planning to drive through Kansas on their way to Colorado. "You have to do business with your life in western Kansas."

Hours upon hours of a landscape so open will expose you, humble you, baffle you. Driving those miles alone, encircled by a sky that only ends when it touches the horizon, a person is either forced to choose distraction with podcasts and sunflower seeds or shut off the noise completely and reckon with the nature of being human.

The sky stretched around me that day like an open canvas. This Kansas sky, the one I always loved as a child, suddenly seemed too empty, devoid of comfort. As I drove down the straight, four-lane interstate, I could see for miles, but I could not imagine more than my next step.

I knew about tornadoes. At least, I knew about the practices of protecting myself from them. I had grown up hearing tornado siren tests in our neighborhood every Wednesday morning. I had rehearsed tornado drills in the hallway at elementary school, my little head tucked beneath my hands with both elbows pointing toward the floor. ("I don't understand how that's going to protect us?" my daughter once told me after practicing a similar drill at school, and I must say I have always wondered the same thing.) I had watched county names roll across the bottom of the television with a characteristic beeping alarm, warning us to take cover. I had spent many long nights in a dark basement huddled around my mom's portable radio as we tracked the path of tornadoes across county lines, waiting for an all-clear.

But until that day in Chapman, I had never experienced a tornado disaster on the ground.

The scene looked exactly like you would expect, yet nothing like you would expect. Tornadoes are vicious, undiscerning beasts, not only ripping things apart but spinning them around and distributing contents everywhere. The tops of houses and trees looked as if someone had taken a giant bite out of them. Much of the school was in piles of bricks and ripped-apart desks. Houses in the hardest-hit part of town stood gaping open, like a terrible version of dollhouses. Others were marked with spray-painted red X's, indicating they had been searched, with many unsafe to reenter.

The summer humidity fell in sticky layers as I walked across a cleared-out park to the volunteer tent. Inside the tent, we were divided into small groups of six to eight people and assigned to different projects. For most of the morning I joined a team wading through debris—shredded desks from the local high school, battered stuffed animals and children's clothing, a busted and ripped-apart recliner. We sorted the items into those that seemed salvageable and those that appeared to be damaged for good.

Our efforts felt meager in the face of the sheer number of things that needed to be sorted, but we focused on one open yard, simply picking up, piling, picking up, piling, picking up, piling.

Inside of such destruction, every scene on which you rest your eyes is full of loss. But during that volunteer shift, I learned that recovery involves the simplest of actions: picking up whatever small piece you can hold in your hands—one piece of wood, one busted-up stuffed animal, one no-longer-working radio—and sorting it into a pile, then moving on to the next.

"It's not gone; I'm just going to keep it for you," my mom said, taking another object out of my hands and placing it inside an open cardboard box.

After driving through western Kansas, I had stopped to stay at my parents' house. Now, my mom sat beside me in the middle of the basement floor, the place where we had once sheltered together from tornadoes during my childhood. Dozens of open boxes I had hastily packed after graduation were scattered around the room, their contents a mystery. My task: sort through my boxes from college and decide what needed to be thrown away, and what should come with me to my new apartment.

Packing is always a terrible chore, made even harder that day because I kept coming across painful memories. I lingered over some items for too long, wondering what to do with them. Keep or toss, keep or toss? My grief made the process more painful and slower than it might have otherwise been. Finally, in some swell of desperation and motherly knowing, my mom grabbed an empty box and set it in front of her. Every time I held an object and flinched at letting it go, she took it from me and placed it inside the box.

Not gone. Just hidden.

Somehow, that was all I needed. She continued to sit beside me that afternoon until all the boxes were emptied, sorted, and repacked—until they had been lightened and rearranged, ready to be loaded back into my car for the next leg of my journey—helping me with the hard work of picking up and putting away.

In literature and popular culture, tornadoes are synonymous with wreckage, but they are also a means to transformation. The most well-known example is *The Wizard of Oz*, of course, in which, at least in the popular reading, Dorothy's tornado is the catalyst for an adventure requiring courage and new friendships. But my favorite example is found in Leif Enger's book *Peace Like a River*, in which the fictional character Jeremiah Land also undergoes a tornado-induced metamorphosis. Jeremiah starts out on the path to becoming a doctor, but one evening he is swept up into a tornado, only to be miraculously discovered again, without a scratch, on a nearby farm.

To his wife's dismay, Jeremiah walks away from his ambition to become a doctor after the tornado. He begins working for a plumber and eventually becomes the janitor at his kids' school. The change is puzzling to everyone, and the decision is costly for him in many ways.

But after the tornado, Jeremiah Land also becomes a sort of healer. A conduit of miracles, you might say.

Jeremiah's son Reuben, the narrator of the story, often expresses confusion that his dad, who is the smartest and most devout person he knows, works in a job so disdained by the boy's peers. The only explanation Jeremiah ever offers him is this: "I was treated so *gently* up there, kids."

Hinge moments, a friend of mine calls them. Points at which your life changes, whether for good or for bad, never to return in quite the same form.

Loss, whether we experience it or merely bear witness to it, changes us, places us at a crossroads so that even if we remain (or, in my case, return) physically where we began, we are no longer quite the same on the inside. My grief that summer was small compared to the losses experienced by the residents of Chapman. But maybe suffering isn't well-measured by size, and instead by the way it compels us on an emotional journey, rearranging our hopes and priorities in big and small ways.

On the clean-up crew in Chapman, I could not sense any changes happening inside my own soul or story, but maybe a sign of my own transformation-in-process was my agreeing to a chore I had never volunteered for before, and that surely would have shocked anyone who knew me at that point in my life: garbage collection.

For hours after lunch, I clung to the back of a full-sized garbage truck with one hand, trying to turn my face away from the stench rising from the back, stopping occasionally to jump off and collect bags of expired milk or rotting meat. Residents had piled the contents of their refrigerators into those bags, quickly going rancid in the searing heat. Our small team tiptoed carefully across downed electrical lines, collecting whatever we could and tossing it in the truck. The streets smelled of sourness and rot.

We wound through the streets for the rest of that hot afternoon, our clothes stained with the juice of leaking food, my arms shaking from the heaviness of hauling bags to the truck. For much of my young life, I had struggled to enter messy places. I preferred to use my mind rather than my hands, and to deal with the tidy rather than the exploded and difficult. But here I was, on a volunteer crew where I knew no one, willingly wearing rotten meat juice. Living inside my own hinge moment.

Fifteen years later, I am driving down I-70 again, this time in a minivan with two curly-haired kids in the backseat. Although I carried them inside of my body for a combined eighteen months, they both came out looking a whole lot like my husband, Brad, and I'm only a little sad about it.

When I announced we were taking a two-hour day trip during their last week of summer vacation, both kids complained.

"Where are we going, Mom? Why are we going there?"

"It's called Chapman," I say, talking as I click on my blinker and switch lanes. "We're going to a place that once got hit by a tornado."

Today, the weather is nearly perfect. The sky is clear and blue, and as we drive, I rehearse the story for them—how a tornado hit Chapman when I was in the middle of a hard season myself, and how I helped with the clean-up efforts. I want to see what the town looks like now, I tell them.

My daughter has questions. "What will it look like? How will we see the tornado?"

I try to explain that the tornado happened long ago, before she was born, so it probably won't look like anything happened at all. Then again, this is my first visit back to Chapman since that day, so I'm not sure what to expect, or if I will even find what I am looking for.

What *am* I looking for, as a grown woman who has traveled miles past her young adult self? Maybe I just want to know for myself that the story of that place has carried on.

"So it is re-builded?" my daughter asks, several times, trying to figure out what this means. It's so hard to understand time as a child, especially when something happened before you were born. I think about myself during that season: young and ambitious—willing to drive alone to a disaster scene—yet wholly unable to understand the long arc of living, to imagine life outside of my immediate experience. I couldn't understand time, either.

When I pull off the interstate at Chapman, the memories immediately come back: the barriers, the check-in, the detour signs. But this time, as we drive into town without any checkpoint to stop us, past the rebuilt middle school and high school and into the center of town, I cannot help but notice its density.

When I was last here, the tornado had swept everything away, carved a wide-open path and leveled everything in the town. It takes me a minute to get my bearings. There are now trees. Houses. Stores and shops.

Then, I see the park.

"There!" I say, maybe more enthusiastic than one would expect to be over a small, square park. "This is where the volunteers set up," I recall.

I pull along the side of the road, and we hop out of the van to see if there is any evidence of that fateful day—and there is.

A new structure stands in the middle of the park—a tornado shelter. On the front, a picture of the woman who died in that storm, along with a memorial. A stone on the edge of the park dedicates the place to the first responders, and a sign in front of the school offices quotes a former city official who declared the city would rebuild. Fifteen years later, reminders of the tornado are everywhere.

I wander around the shelter taking a few pictures, marveling how things can look so normal on this sunny day, yet how the memory of the tornado is still woven into the fabric of this place. The people here have walked through immense pain, and now they have physically built reminders, marking what happened and how they came through.

They have, as my daughter said, *rebuilded.*

After driving around Chapman for a few minutes (it's a small town, so it doesn't take long), my kids and I get back on the interstate and drive another ten minutes to the nearby city of Abilene. Since we're only ninety minutes from my hometown at this point, my mom has come to meet us for lunch. She is fifteen years older, too, now not a mom comforting her adult child, but a beloved grandma my kids call Nana.

The minute we park on the sidewalk, my daughter catches a glimpse of my mom standing down the street. She doesn't even ask if she can leave my side—she simply takes off. Full throttle, legs stretching out, hair trailing behind her, she runs toward the sight of her Nana standing in the doorway of a small-town restaurant.

I stand and watch to make sure she is safe, marveling at the sheer joy pulsing through her little body. I laugh out loud as she sprints an entire city block toward the woman who is so special to both of us, the same woman who has witnessed the most confusing and tender pieces of my story, and who taught me how to shelter and clean up from many storms.

And now my own daughter is sprinting down the sidewalk toward her, her love and joy contagious, her hair blowing in a Kansas wind that is, for today, not destructive, but full of hope for the future.

Passing with Care

On building a life on a landscape

"The best I can ask for is that this love, which has been built on countless failures, will continue to grow."
—Madeleine L'Engle, *The Irrational Season*

Brad and I are headed west on I-70 one Saturday afternoon, cruising just past Salina. The open four-lane road is beginning to shift from pencil straight to slightly winding as we enter the Smoky Hills, an expanse that extends across the sedimentary deposits of north-central Kansas and reaches into southern Nebraska. Like the Flint Hills, this area defies the myth of geographic flatness, its sandstone outcrops carpeted over by prairie grasses and bushy trees. Today, as on most days, prevailing south winds fold the grasses into half-bend poses, and although it is only late May, the sun is hot enough to be spilling little pools of imaginary water across the lanes ahead.

Brad, who will be my husband in just two weeks, sits at the steering wheel of my white Toyota Corolla. His usually curly blond hair is trimmed short, and he is wearing khaki pants and a dress shirt. I am in the passenger's seat wearing a sundress, jewelry, and high heels, with the ends of my hair gently curled. Behind us, plastic tubs and boxes are stacked into the narrow back seat, along with a suitcase carrying an unorganized tangle of sunscreen, flip-flops, and swimsuits for our upcoming honeymoon in Mexico. The tubs gently jostle back and forth as we drive, slow dancing to the quiet tune of Ray LaMontagne from the car's CD player.

This is a big day for us, but we are not headed to our wedding—not yet. First, we will attend Brad's cousin's wedding in the little town of Ellsworth, Kansas, the final wedding on the calendar before our own. Then, it will be our turn to set our sights on our future together.

We have only been engaged for six months, but the days until our wedding have inched by, as they always do when you're waiting for something wonderful. I have recently finished a spring semester teaching *The Taming of the Shrew*, Shakespeare's comedy about the fiery marriage of Petruchio and Katherina, to high school sophomores. Each day during the preceding fourth quarter, I slowly walked five classes through Early Modern English and the tangling web of characters, then returned home and spent my evenings in a flurry of distance wedding planning, paper grading, and decision-making about graduate school. Finally, over two short days, I packed up my entire high school classroom, placing all the sweat and work from my early years of teaching into crates, along with extra file folders and my collection of Shakespeare. After handing in my classroom keys, I stayed up all night, packing everything from my apartment into boxes as well.

Now, as we drive west, all the stressors and exhaustion are overshadowed by hopefulness. I have reached a threshold between before and after, cruising ahead into a new phase of life with the man I love. Ahead of us spreads a cloudless windshield of vibrant, robin's-egg blue—the color of something new. Nothing could make me wonder about more mundane things, like whether in the last two years I have ever changed the oil in my car.

But as we crest a little hill, rolling along at seventy-five miles per hour, Brad announces that the engine light has come on the dashboard.

"Huh," I say, thinking little of it.

Then, almost as quickly as the warning light has appeared, Ray LaMontagne abruptly pauses his crooning. The air conditioner quits blowing across my sundress, and the lights on the CD player disappear.

The car takes on a sudden quietness as our speed decelerates, the engine no longer having power to crest the next hill.

"The engine just died," Brad says, calmly. He does not frantically yell, as I might have, "What do I do?" Instead, he peers down at the dashboard and slowly guides the car toward the shoulder of the interstate.

The Corolla rolls to a decisive halt on a gentle slope of road. No gas stations, no restaurants, no little clustered buildings are in sight, not even in the spacious view this section of prairie has granted. Semi-trucks and other cars continue to cruise by, and I suddenly feel the speed at which they are driving and the sensation of being firmly at a standstill. It's vulnerable, being stopped here when everything else is moving so quickly.

Brad gets out to investigate under the hood while I wait in the car, hoping for a quick fix, since we are already running late. But I soon realize it's far too hot to keep the door shut without the air conditioner running, so I push open the passenger door. Searing heat rises from the asphalt, but the Kansas wind nudges the edge of my sundress, convincing me the prairie is a better place to wait than inside the car. I climb out and wade a few steps into the shin-deep grass, balancing on my beige heels before lowering myself onto the side of the ditch.

In the distance, enormous white turbines line the hills, their white blades rhythmically rotating. We have broken down near the Smoky Hills Wind Farm, currently the largest wind farm in the state of Kansas. Wind farming is currently exploding across the Midwest, an attempt to draw energy from one of the most consistent resources of the Great Plains. Often, I have passed a wide-load semi with an extra-long bed carrying a single turbine blade. Just one of those blades is as long as four or five lengths of my car. Now the enormous blades slowly rotate clockwise, powered by the same breeze sending curled hair across my nose and chin.

Debates will rage for years over wind farms like this one, with some residents disdaining their unsightliness on the open landscape, and others welcoming the cash flow offered by their development. These conversations surface the complexity and extent of all sorts of regional crises—prairie ecosystems wrestling for life alongside struggling rural communities alongside the increasingly burdened air we all breathe.

Crises of all sorts have played out on this landscape. Today, we are caught inside a small one of our own, unable to get where we wish to go. I sit outside of my broken-down, gas-powered vehicle, no longer able to contribute to the air pollution, and wish I could harness the wind's power to propel us forward. Instead, I must repeatedly push hair out of my face and wrestle the breeze against the skirt of my dress. A fly tries to land on my leg, then quickly sails off with a gust. Prairie insects pop and sizzle in the grass.

After several minutes, Brad comes around the side of the car, looking resigned. He plops down next to me, draping his arms over his knees.

"I don't know what's wrong," he sighs. "We need to call someone."

We phone my dad, who instructs us to contact a service station in Salina (a specific service station, because he knows the businesses in this region), and begins driving toward us to help. Then, we can do nothing but sit—two engaged lovers all dressed up for a wedding, hanging out on an interstate ditch in the middle of the prairie, fighting off the wind while pitting out our dress clothes, looking like we have come to view a performance in a roadside amphitheater, one of slowly spinning turbines against the broad backdrop of sky.

Brad is a Kansas kid, too—more of a small-town kid than me, his dad having farmed for years in western Kansas when he was young. We have broken down not far from the small town where he attended high school, near farms where he spent long afternoons and summer days outside, helping area farmers with chores and harvest, growing up alongside the land's yearly rhythms.

We both have many stories from our early lives in this place. Now, we are beginning to write them together. Over time, it will begin to feel fitting that before we fully set out on our married life, we must sit together, unmoving. After all, there are many stories yet unwritten—days and drives in which we will want to move forward, but instead will break down, stop, or need to call for help. We will face our own small and large crises and learn to navigate them beside each other.

"At least we have something to watch," I say, as the blades move in the unending wind. The low hills rise beneath the base of each turbine, anchoring them steadily to the ground.

———

I don't remember the exact moment we begin driving McDowell Creek Road together. I believe it's on a Sunday afternoon, about one year after our breakdown on I-70, when we are living in Manhattan, Kansas, returning to our college town for graduate school and work. One day, as we are navigating the strange, open space between church and homework and laundry, experiencing some Sunday blues about the week ahead, Brad turns off onto the exit. "Have you driven this before?" he asks.

There are two main exits off I-70 to reach Manhattan: exit 303 and exit 313. These are the exits I most often take, chosen for speed and timing. Both are lovely drives, winding through the hills, offering sunset views and scenic overlooks. I especially love the overlook off Highway 177, which features the Flint Hills in all its glory—grasses unfolding in shadows and lines of greens, purples, and blues.

But between the more well-worn exits, the other road to the interstate is a quieter, more meandering path that follows parts of the Kansas River until it turns into the streams of McDowell Creek, or County Highway 901. This is the road in between—the journey to take if you are not in a hurry. Or, if you are a young, twenty-something married couple out for a Sunday drive, it is the road to take while trying to figure out your life together. When I was younger, I often poked fun at older couples out on afternoon drives, moving more slowly than I wished. But now, these drives seem appealing to me—even essential.

Brad and I had married in my hometown on a summer evening, two weeks after the engine failure. We held our reception in the ballroom of a twelve-story former hotel turned senior living center. That night, a ferocious storm in the area sent some guests leaving the reception just as the party was getting started, and I hoped for no tornado warnings so we could dance instead of sheltering in the basement with residents who lived on the other eleven floors. Mercifully, the storm did not send us beneath ground that night, and we carried on with dancing and cake and youthful fanfare. But if rain on your wedding day is good luck, perhaps a Kansas thunderstorm is just the deluge we needed.

We moved into a narrow row apartment and filled the kitchen with new plates, as-yet unchipped or stained or dropped by future children or us. We filled our days with fresh opportunities. I studied theories and wrote and taught thesis statements (so many thesis statements). He studied circuits and completed mysterious-to-me paperwork called submittals (so many submittals). We lived on a blend of optimism, young love, disillusionment, and overconfidence. We thought we knew some things because we were college graduates and young professionals, but we didn't know how young we were, because the knowledge of youth is an awareness you receive in reverse.

Our first fight was over a shower curtain, a floral one I ordered to cover the laundry area in our kitchen. He walked inside after work and declared it ugly, and right then, we learned how stubborn we could both be. I am apparently most stubborn, because that curtain would remain featured in three of our homes over the course of ten years, until I finally retired it, tattered thin with holes and fingerprints from the children.

We were happy, and sometimes, also lonely. Loneliness is surprising to a newly married couple because we are all sold a script that our other half should complete us, perhaps even make us new, but of course that's not how it works. A marriage partnership is more like a long journey, one in which you must blend disparate paths and personalities and stories together. Across many years, contexts, and landscapes, we would need to more fully understand each other. We would need to navigate not only crises, but also mundane, ordinary living.

Early on, we discovered that we talk best while in some sort of motion: walking or driving. So that first afternoon drive on McDowell Creek Road turns into several, eventually becoming an unspoken ritual. When we don't know what else to do, or when we need to sort something out, we intuitively head to McDowell Creek. The two-lane road initially leads through a scenery of bushy trees, past the exit to Pillsbury Crossing, where you can wade out into a shallow creek and crawl across rocks, plus a few small businesses and houses. Then, the landscape begins to open up. Small farms dot the flat valley along the riverbed, while the low hills of the Konza Prairie rise in the distance. We follow the gentle turns of the two-lane road, staring outside the window as we chat, passing time, talking and not talking at all, simply being together.

We pass hills peppered with limestone characteristic to the region, small grain elevators, farmhouses with low silos and cattle resting in the shade. In autumn, we pass along the rusty earth in oranges, yellows, and reds. In summer, we pass green trees spilling along both sides of the road. We pass beneath clear skies and cloudy ones, all along the same route to the interstate, where we turn around and drive back toward the city, following the same road, again. We are not really going anywhere. We are simply companioning each other, working our way through our early life by watching the landscape as it passes.

"Pass with Care," several signs say, indicating a section of the two-lane curving road where passing is allowed. Two-lane roads are precarious, especially narrow, curving ones in our speed-ridden era, where one slow tractor or semi can send impatient drivers careening into the other lane without knowing what's around the bend, whether oncoming traffic or a darting deer in the dark. Passing is always a risk.

But that is what we are learning to do—to pass through all seasons and types of weather, on spacious roads as well as narrow ones, through the breakdowns and engine failures, the fights and repair. As a beloved therapist will remind us many times in a later season of our marriage, *unconditional love is the engine. Love fuels.*

More important than remembering to change the oil in my car—which I know now is very important—our life together must unfold not just over a foundation of soil and grass and hills and flat land, but on a bedrock of safety, security, and love, a landscape we must create and tend together.

The Red Tree

On finding beauty during loss

"To open ourselves to love is to expose ourselves to the Great Asterisk that renders every love—large or small, person or passion—vulnerable to the terrible risks of loss. Love and loss are always closer than we'd care to confess."
—Stephanie Duncan Smith, *Even After Everything*

Brad and I move across town into a rental house with a small, sloping backyard, which descends into something akin to a forest. I have never lived in an area so densely populated with trees, but here in the northern Flint Hills, tall trees and dense foliage cover my entire backyard as cardinals, wood finches, and tiny sparrows flit through their branches.

I am brimming with early life, too. One afternoon in late July, during the summer after I finish graduate school, Brad leaves on a work trip in Alabama. I come home from my job on campus and move the recliner directly in front of the window air conditioning unit, just as I have every night for the past twelve weeks, trying to melt away the heat and nausea. Outside the living room windows, those leafy trees overtake our backyard, creating a cocoon for the back half of the house. That night, I fall asleep in the quiet, to only the sound of the whirring air conditioner.

But at three o'clock in the morning, I begin calling Brad's phone repeatedly.

Rrrrrring.

Rrrrrring.

We are in our late twenties, still unfamiliar with middle-of-the-night interruptions. Before he left, I never even thought to ask the name of the hotel where he would be staying. I know only that he is in some city in Alabama with his cell phone turned to its usual nighttime mode of "silent."

Between unanswered calls, I shuffle to the bathroom and watch blood drip into the toilet, tiny crimson tendrils sinking and spiraling through the water toward a network of pipes and plumbing below.

I rehearse the sounds I heard three days ago—a quickly paced *ta-dum*, *ta-dum*, like a miniature racehorse, followed by a doctor's voice, "Everything looks great." Now, a doctor's voice speaks to me again over the phone, instructing me to wait at home until the clinic opens at nine.

Six more hours. Fifteen more trips to the bathroom. Another series of unanswered *rrrings* and wondering whether any noise still sounds inside my abdomen.

July bleeds into August, and I lie on the couch watching the London Olympics with my mom, who has driven several hours to keep me company. After that first long and lonely night, I had rushed to the clinic as soon as it opened and heard, yet again, a hopeful *ta-dum, ta-dum.*

But now, as the Olympic rendition of "Chariots of Fire" plays in the background, the doctor speaks to me over the phone, saying words like "increased nuchal fold" and "genetic testing" and "something might be wrong."

"I'm so sorry," the doctor tells me. "But all you can do is wait."

The hours pass slowly; the tendrils keep falling. I sit again in front of the tree-lined windows and watch the American women gymnasts win a gold medal. Brad promises never to leave his phone on silent mode again, and we make decisions about genetic testing from seven hundred miles apart. My mom makes sandwiches and forces me to eat, but I lie alone in bed at night and listen to the *whirr* of the air conditioner, blurring together with the sound of my fear.

Brad returns home from his trip on Friday night, and by the next morning, I am doubled over on the bathroom floor in pain, tendrils turning into red vines climbing out of my body. Brad scoops me up and drives me to the hospital, where the ultrasound machine confirms the news I have feared: *silence.*

I visit the labor and delivery wing of the hospital for the first time that day, delivering myself over to a whirlwind of medical conversations, anesthesia, and recovery instructions. When a kind nurse pushes me out to the car in a wheelchair hours later, she tries to offer me some encouragement. "I think you'll be back here soon, under better circumstances," she says.

But that night, I am simply back in the recliner with the backyard forest behind me, watching the Olympics with Brad, trying to numb my grief through the repeated refrain of "Chariots of Fire" and the ongoing noise of the window unit.

Whirr, whirr.

As August continues, I put on my suit jacket and return to work. I am soothed by sounds of life beginning to return to campus. On the first day of the semester, I welcome a class of new students to a special section of freshman English, a writing class that doubles as a first-year seminar.

"The first semester of college can be an adjustment," I say, handing out the syllabus. "But I'm here to be a resource for you."

I pour myself into teaching and into training older students to mentor first-year students. I wear a business suit and heels to meetings where we talk about how fragile the first semester of college life can be and discuss strategies for retaining students.

But when I shed my work clothes and lay in bed at night, I am haunted by what I could not retain. One night in the darkness, I nudge Brad awake. "Hon," I whisper. "I don't know where our baby is."

He slits his eyes open. "What do you mean?"

"I—I don't know exactly when I lost it."

"It's okay," he says, wrapping one arm around me and pulling me closer. "It's okay. You don't have to know."

His deep breathing resumes, blending with the ongoing *whirr* of the window unit. I place my ear on his chest and listen for his heartbeat. The collective weight of our bodies creates a pool in the middle of the mattress, and I anchor myself to the steady rhythm of blood pumping through his body, trying not to fall into the network of pipes and plumbing below.

Ta-dum, ta-dum.

August melts into September. The trees are still green, but the air is growing less heavy. Nearly every Saturday I visit the farmers market and come home with a small bouquet of flowers for our kitchen table, tending them and taking comfort in their fleeting yet beautiful lives. It feels good to care for these living things, if only for a short time.

One day after work, I walk down a large hill from campus in my heels, finally beginning to feel some sense of steadiness again. The marching band is practicing in the distance, the sound of brass instruments and bass drums floating across campus.

Brad is sitting in our car at the bottom of the hill, waiting to drive me home. But when I get in the car, he doesn't start driving right away.

"I need to tell you something," he says, his voice serious. "I can't keep going like this."

"Um. What do you mean?"

"Not us. Just—this. Life."

I listen from the passenger's seat as he tells me how he has been experiencing an ongoing, low-grade depression for months, even before the miscarriage. He describes feeling overwhelmed and numb, each day bleeding into the gray of the next.

Over the next few weeks, we talk about counseling and doctor's visits, wonder about job changes or possible moves. I am there, but I absorb many of our conversations quietly, unsure how to process all the new information I have been given.

"You're not really helping," he tells me one night.

"I'm sorry," I say, glancing at the drawer where I have just stuffed all the ultrasound pictures. "I don't know how to help." The miles we have traveled separately over the past months stretch out between us. I want to be able to help him, but in my quieter moments, I can only hear the sound on the other end of the phone at 3:00 AM: *silence.*

September becomes October, and cooler weather finally starts to sink its fingers into the Midwest. Most of the trees are still holding onto their green, with some beginning to give way to yellow. But the air no longer sits heavy; the weight of humidity has lifted.

I celebrate my birthday that month, and Brad and I end the day by going on a quiet evening walk through the neighborhood. We are still carrying our individual griefs, but we are trying to find a way forward, together.

As we turn a corner, I spot red crawling up a small sugar maple tree—its brilliant color standing out in a landscape of still-green and yellow leaves.

"Beautiful!" I gasp, walking toward the tree. The tree is in a stranger's yard, but I step across the curb and onto the front lawn without caring what the neighbors think. I only want to be close to whatever has made this tree turn so fully toward the shifting air. I stand under the tree and look at its crimson leaves. Several have already fallen and spread out across the grass, dotting the ground with color. I know the tree is in a season of loss, but right now, I simply take in its beauty.

"Here, turn around," Brad says from the middle of the road, holding his phone up like a camera. "I'll take your picture."

He is not usually one to suggest impromptu photo shoots, and I am not exactly prepared for a picture, but it is my birthday. So, standing on the curb of a random stranger's house, with my arms hanging awkwardly to my side and my shirt twisted sideways, I turn toward him and offer a cheesy smile.

Click.

We have more miles to travel together before we will fully understand each other's pain from these months. But with the onset of cooler weather, we can finally switch off the air conditioner and open up all the windows. Outside, the wind makes a gentle *whish* as it passes through the small backyard forest. As leaves across the hills release from their branches, I hold on to that picture of the red tree and the girl beneath it, trying to believe beauty can still be present in the midst of loss.

How to See the Sky from the City

On still searching for space

"Feel the sky."
—Luci Shaw, "The Weight of Air"

Buy a house in Kansas City when you're eight months pregnant. When your body has morphed into a creature that is half-woman, half-baby, and steam is starting to rise from summer sidewalks and gooey sweat droplets are sliding down your back while your stomach lurches beyond your control, you will not have time to walk around the fading, three-story house and assess its view of the sky from every angle. You only want to know how soon you can begin painting the nursery.

Begin painting when the ink is still wet on your mortgage paperwork. When you rush to grab a new paintbrush wearing only your socks and tumble down the hardwood staircase, earning a bruise in the shape of Ohio on your side-butt, forsake your project. Take your lumbering, limping self to the outdoor gardens of a nearby art museum.

While there, find yourself always lingering near the highest point of the gardens, wishing you could float your pregnant frame up over the sculptures, over the trees, and take the form of a cloud. But since you cannot hop, much less float, sink your weight into that spot. Learn exactly where to stand on the brick path and how the ground in that place feels beneath your feet. Find out where you can plant yourself to see as much of the city sky as possible.

This is a sacred space.

You will return here often with a stroller in tow, when your arms feel heavy with a sleepless newborn and your brain is sinking into fog like quicksand. The harder you try to become a perfect mom, the faster your lungs feel like they are filling with dirt. But being under the sky helps you breathe. You can lean your thoughts onto something much larger than yourself, like a hammock from above. You never knew how much you needed the open skies of your childhood—that Kansas sky looming around you in panorama—until you left it just a few miles behind.

As you have now discovered, the home where you rock and nurse your new baby all day has a lousy view of the sky, from all angles, so you must get creative. In the afternoons, put your nap-resisting baby in his car seat and take long drives around the city, traveling to the point where you can see blue stretching directly onto green, instead of onto rooftops or stone. Then, when the baby falls asleep, pull into a parking lot.

Parking lots are also sacred spaces.

It seems counterintuitive, when you are surrounded by people buying groceries and pushing carts and looking down at their three-inch screens instead of up. But when the developers who bought this land were carving over the earth with wide swaths of concrete, they were also making you a clearer viewing place. As much as you despise concrete, you will learn to appreciate these gray ponds in the middle of the city.

At about 5:45 PM during the winter months, when you can tell from the cracks between houses that the thinning air is refracting light into shades of pink and orange and deep purple—and if your husband is walking in the door, and if your now two children are not crying, and if it seems everyone will be content eating mac and cheese for dinner—unwind yourself from the chaos, sprint to your car, and race the sunset to the nearest grocery store.

Pray to catch the four stoplights just right, silently yell at a few shoppers to move out of your way, and pull into a spot facing west. You may have missed the brightest colors—the pink is already turning to peach, and the clouds have already faded from coral to dark gray—but catching any part of this daily showing is better than none. Stare at the sky like a drive-in movie-goer, in awe that this show is different every night.

When you return home ten minutes later, you will be a little nicer to everyone, and they will be glad you made your pilgrimage to the nearest parking lot.

Over time, as you pay attention to your compulsions to watch the sky, and as you realize that not everyone chases beauty in the land of grocery shoppers, you will reach the conclusion that perhaps you are one of those creative types. You are a writer—one who needs to see the sky, but still lives in a house with a terrible view of the sky.

But writers thrive in less-than-ideal conditions! So, again, get creative. Make a writing space for yourself in the attic, on the third floor. You will need to take up a yoga practice to support the way your neck aches from pressing your face against the window, craning your head backwards, trying to see past trees and A-frame rooftops, searching for triangles of blue fading into gray into white.

Even so, this is another sacred space.

Like seeing the sky, writing allows you to breathe. You ascend the stairs leading to your own thoughts and words the way water runs downstream, always searching for the larger substance from which you came.

As you write stories, and as you write about your own childhood, you will again remember the appeal of that Kansas sky. Begin to regularly drive thirty or forty-five minutes outside of the city into Kansas, where the view of the sky is unobstructed by buildings and wires and people.

When you're there, take pictures. The tiny screen on your phone will become filled with pictures—photos you'll need when you are writing about the sky at your desk, trying to remember what it looks like at different times, in different places, at different times of day. A three-inch view of the horizon is always better than none.

And on days when you cannot drive toward the sky, revisit the art museum gardens, returning to that space on the hill. Occasionally, wander inside the museum and stand in front of Monet's *Water Lilies*. The more time you spend trying to see and describe the sky, the more you begin to understand why Monet painted so many of those water lilies, in so many different types of light, at so many different times of day.

So keep writing about the sky and talking about the sky. Make your family and friends tired of hearing you talk and write about the sky. If you talk about it enough, and if you annoy them enough, they will become recruits on your sky-seeking quest. Your husband will wake you up early one morning on vacation because the sun is rising into layers of pink and gold, and he knows you would not want to miss it. Your kids will run into the house whenever the clouds are making a funny shape and yell at you to "come outside!" as though they have just witnessed fireworks. At dinner one evening, they will inform you that they have been planning special events for Mother's Day, and they know just the activity for you—family cloud-watching.

As you watch the clouds from your backyard, through the small square of sky overhead, surrounded by your family and your sagging, three-story house, feel yourself begin to breathe.

This, too, is a sacred space.

The Cottonwood Standing by the Highway

On following the seeds of calling

"The writer operates at a peculiar crossroads where time and place and eternity somehow meet. His problem is to find that location."
—Flannery O'Connor, *Mystery and Manners*

"Honk, Mom!"

We are cruising around a curve on K-96 highway, and I am in the driver's seat, taking my kids to visit my parents' house.

I press the horn of the minivan two times—*meep, meep*—just as my parents did when we drove around this same curve in my childhood. An oncoming car in the other lane honks too. My kids cheer.

We are participating in a long-standing tradition—honking at the old cottonwood tree on the side of the road. The cottonwood is the state tree of Kansas, and this particular cottonwood has become a sort of patron saint in the area, receiving daily honks for luck, ribbons to commemorate grief or celebration, local newspaper articles written on its behalf, even a Facebook following.

Its branches stately yet drooping, its trunk bearing the signs of weathered years, this cottonwood has survived storms, droughts, and progress. When the highway expanded from two lanes into four during the mid-1990s, the tree was supposed to be removed. But after local public outcry, the highway was rerouted just to the north, and the tree was saved.

During the same highway expansion, part of Grandpa Don's farm, several miles down this same road, was not as fortunate.

"Pond's looking full," I say as we pass the farm. The property once sat back farther from the road, but now, it sits right along the highway. "Must've gotten some decent rain this year."

"Are we there yet?" one kid whines from the back seat.

"Not yet—almost," I answer. "Just twenty more minutes to Nana's."

But as we cruise past the farm at seventy-five miles per hour, I am thinking of a little patch of land hidden beneath these four lanes of traffic, a place I used to explore as a kid. I wonder if the answer is actually, *yes, we are.*

Suddenly, I am ten years old, crawling across rocks with my cousins until we reach the place where the pond narrows into a penciled stream. On the old two-lane highway in the distance, cars pass in metronomic time, their sound overpowered by the Kansas wind circling my frame, unsettling and re-balancing me with its strong arms.

Perched on a small boulder, I lift my arms into the shape of a "T" and let the wind pull me toward each end of the sky. I could run for miles in either direction, and I would never reach the elusive space where sky meets curving earth. Suspended here, my young life stretched between the horizon, my imagination leans into the wind and propels me toward my own future at the speed of limitless time.

I could go anywhere from right here.

"I always imagine you on a quest," my therapist tells me during one of our sessions.

I laugh, picturing myself sitting on a horse in the middle of the city, with a knight's shield in one hand and a diaper bag full of wipes and snacks slung over my other shoulder, yelling at Siri to give me directions to the nearest playground. If this is a quest, it has not led me through an enchanted forest or magical kingdom, but straight into the stuff of ordinary life.

Later, I look up the definition of "quest" to confirm my suspicion: the word comes from the same root as "question," from the Latin word meaning "to ask or seek."

My question: *Where am I going?*

This question compelled me to show up in therapy in the first place, and a year later, the same question keeps me returning, still asking what it might mean to live out of a deeper sense of calling. But to answer that question, it seems I need to spend more time with this one: *Where have I gone?*

I feel like I am sitting in front of a big pile of memories from my past, and I'm slowly sorting through them, only to be handed more questions. Why have I always felt the need to be seen as responsible? Why did I think I needed to do something "important"? In the past, did I achieve things to be seen? To be loved? What really brought me joy as a kid—and does it matter? Do I think *I* matter, even when I don't have answers, even when I am covered in residue from sticky fingers and snot from tiny noses?

The questions swirl and lift as I go about my ordinary days of mothering and teaching. I have a few answers—answers I have been told or given—but now I must learn to live them out. I must once again lean onto the strong arms of the wind and see where they lead.

My Grandpa Don dies of brain cancer that spring, during months in which I have started to fumble my way through writing for fun again, playing with poetry and creative words instead of only academic ones, giving myself permission to string words and images together during nap time or while cooking dinner.

We gather for my grandpa's funeral in the small-town church he attended most of his life and bury him just down the highway from the farm. The evening after his funeral, I am sitting at a drop-leaf table in my grandparents' living room, both leaves stretched wide, covered with pictures and memorabilia from my grandpa's life, when I notice a small book called *My Pomes.* It's a collection of poetry written by Grandpa Don's mother, my Great Grandma Mary.

My uncle compiled Great Grandma Mary's poetry from her journals after her death and gave them to the family as Christmas gifts. I'm pretty sure I've seen this little book sitting on a shelf in my childhood bedroom, but I have never cared to read it.

Now, I open it up.

The introduction describes a story I have heard but remember only vaguely. In 1924, when Great Grandma Mary was a young teenager, her mom died of breast cancer. My uncle writes that young Mary was woken up in the middle of the night by her father and quoted the Twenty-Third Psalm all the way to the hospital, rehearsing a passage she learned from her now-dying mother. I don't know what kind of car Mary rode in that day, but I picture her in an old farm vehicle, traveling twenty miles between the farm and the same city where I would later be born, a similar route I have just driven with my kids, weeping and fearful, trying to calm herself with words from the King James Bible.

"The LORD is my shepherd, I shall not want."

Were there any sheep living on the family farm, then? Was Mary a shepherd in some way, herself? As a girl, I often saw sheep grazing on the farm, munching the grass like lawn mowers, dropping their smelly pellets across the ground and scattering out of the way whenever a truck approached. But whether Mary knew sheep or not, she certainly knew the green-brown-gold pastures of a central Kansas farm, the quiet waters of a tiny pond, the words of a psalm her mother had knitted into her mind—a mother who had been suddenly snatched from this life.

They laid her mother's body inside a green pasture and piled it with dirt. Things would only get harder for Grandma Mary. Just one year later, her father died, too, after a bout with the flu. At the age of sixteen, Mary, an orphan, was sent to live with a relative.

Great Grandma Mary died when I was five, so I have scant memories of her, and only from visiting her when she was in her nineties, living in a nursing home that smelled of ammonia and old age. I have a brief memory of standing next to her bed as a young girl, tiptoeing toward the edge to say hello at my parents' request. The sight of an elderly person can be terrifying when you're so young. What hard or intrusive questions might they ask? Would they try to touch your hair or your shoulder? I remember hesitating to come too close.

But as I hold the book of poetry before me, I have a sudden desire to know this woman with such a tragic yet remarkable story. I open to the first poem, titled "My Old Piano."

> I played when I lost them, both parents,
> The music was dreary and slow;
> My moods, as the years past, were sounded
> In harmony with response from my soul.

I try to imagine the grief of losing both parents during such formative years, and I watch her work out her profound loss on the piano, through her rhythmic words.

After attending college, Great Grandma Mary got married, and returned with her new husband to her childhood farm. So, as it turns out, the farm off K-96 highway I have always called "Grandpa Don's farm" is really "Great Grandma Mary's farm." Great Grandma Mary, the musician and poet.

The poem continues with her playing the piano as her kids grow up, and eventually getting a new piano. But, she writes, "the old one's shape still shadows."

I ponder that line. Great Grandma Mary's "shape still shadows" too, it seems, in her poetry.

Over the next few days, I read through the rest of her poems. Her poetry is simple, made entirely from the stuff of ordinary life—chaotic mornings sending children off to school, her disdain for dirty dishes, the snow, the squirrels, her kids and grandkids. She writes about her faith, about grief and growing older, and later, about missing those chaotic mornings with her children.

I text some friends to tell them about my discovery. "My Great Grandma wrote this poem about dirty dishes," I say, sending them a photo of her words. "I laughed because I can relate."

"I am not surprised to learn you come from a line of writers," someone writes back.

But I am surprised. The discovery of Great Grandma Mary's poetry feels like a hopeful seed during a time when I am opening myself up to words again, trying to understand what it means to follow stories without understanding where they are going. In a way, this woman I have hardly known becomes famous to me. Not in a glamorous way, but her poetry feels famous the way Naomi Shihab Nye describes in her poem "Famous," in which the poem's speaker complicates the idea of fame itself. Echoing Nye's poetic style, I might say:

> An old woman's poetry is famous
> to her great-granddaughter.
> The cottonwood tree standing by the highway
> is famous to drivers who honk.
> A tiny creek is famous
> to a ten-year-old girl
> long after it has been paved over
> by concrete.

———

Back on my porch in the city, I have my laptop open, and I am thinking of writing when a cottonwood seed lands on the computer and rolls into the crevices of the keys. The tiny seed lodges itself between the Q and the W, and I retrieve it, holding the seed in my hand. The small white seed is pointed like an arrow or a spade, and its cottony wings spread like vining arms. Those thin arms will give the seed its only chance to catch the wind, to find good soil on which to land, to grow roots.

I know the seed's chances of becoming a cottonwood tree here in the city are slim. The one tree from which it came has just released millions of seeds, and only a handful will find the right conditions for growth.

When Grandpa Don was near the end of his life, I thought often about images of trees in the poetry of the Hebrew psalms: trees full of life in old age, trees planted by the water. And now I wonder if those words might have anything to do with the old cottonwood tree planted along the highway, the poetry woven into my family tree, or a young girl with her arms stretched wide into a T.

I open my hand and release the seed, letting it catch the wind. It swirls off the porch, just out of my sight. I cannot quite see where it lands.

Farm Road

On searching and surprise

"Every place has its own beauty."
—Anthony Doerr, *Four Seasons in Rome*

The dirt road leading to my in-laws' farmhouse exists, just like the earth itself exists, but if you don't know where to look, you will never find it.

"So, if I just passed the church, did I miss it?" I have asked my father-in-law over the phone more times than I would care to admit, aimlessly driving down a blacktop road surrounded by open fields and small farms, wondering which gravel road leads to the right place.

I can hear his tone shift predictably throughout the call—first, concern as he tries to figure out exactly where I am, then amusement as he tells me I have missed it, again. And when I finally arrive at the farm safely, there is always the expected bit of gentle teasing.

"Jenna, haven't you been here before?" he asks.

I laugh, realizing that although I've been in the family for over a decade, I still must go searching for my in-laws' house. Perhaps it is my poor sense of direction, or maybe there are just places in the world for which we must always search—places that feel a bit more wonderful because they are hidden.

But if you go searching long enough, or know right where to look, in the middle of a Sedgwick county road, a few miles past the white cross of a country church, an otherwise uninteresting dirt road leads to a small, fifteen-acre plot of land—the meager remains of a much larger section that was farmed and owned by my husband's family for generations until it was sold. Now, the property consists of a large gray-and-white farmhouse, a few scattered barns, an old tin silo, a shop, and a handful of semi-truck beds used for storage. Visitors are eagerly greeted by a rowdy farm dog who sometimes sleeps inside a fence repurposed from an old chicken coup, where hens used to lay delicious eggs before my father-in-law went on an extended vacation and, instead of asking someone to take care of the chickens, decided it was "time to sell 'em."

Even without the chatter of the chickens, that dirt road is both as wonderful and unassuming as a fallen leaf in autumn. The road exists merely as a matter of utility, cutting through the middle of a section of crop acres and leading to several houses. It is surrounded by flat fields, straight, two-lane paved roads intersecting in perfect gridlines, irrigation systems and scattered tree rows designed to protect the crops from wind. The road doesn't have a name to call its own. The handful of residents use the nearby blacktop as an address, and mail only arrives because the local mailman is willing to drive out of his way.

Despite the road's lack of prestige, a simple, seasonal beauty surrounds it. In the spring, green wheat pokes up like grass and quickly sprouts into stems dotted with ladybugs who protect the crop from other insects. As the steamier days of summer arrive, the wheat slowly ripens into dusty gold until the road is lined on both sides by a bushy field of yellow. Then, in one fell swoop during a week in mid-summer, harvest combines hack off the heads of grain and leave only stubble behind. The stubble slowly slumps over until the ground is tilled and replanted, and as the cold days of late autumn return, frost glazes the dirt and covers the buried winter wheat.

Often, on our journeys here from Kansas City, we find the farmhouse full of relatives who have come to greet us. The house has long been a gathering place for holidays, open to any family or friends in the area, or sometimes even lesser-known acquaintances. Whole housefuls once came for every holiday, carrying side dishes to share, writing their names on red Solo cups, eating in each available room and swapping stories. Although the numbers have slowed and trickled as the years have gone on, this is still a gathering place. Several years ago, my father-in-law expanded and replaced the smaller kitchen with a long bar, which becomes filled with a potluck of dishes—baked chicken, veggie trays, and three different types of casseroles (corn casserole, green bean casserole, potato casserole), plus far too many cookies and pies. For those few days, the farmhouse is bustling with people and conversation.

I have grown to love our visits there, and the way I am invited into the hodgepodge mix of people, food, and games. Still, I am an introvert, and I often have an impulse much like Madeleine L'Engle describes of her family's visits to Crosswicks, their New England summer home. Although L'Engle adores her time at Crosswicks, she shares in her book *A Circle of Quiet* that she occasionally retreats from the house full of noise to steal away into the solitude of the natural world where she can be more fully herself. L'Engle's words have freed me on more than one occasion, reminding me that I can dearly love people and still need to withdraw. My current daily life is so dense, full of caretaking and noise and people and sirens and traffic. In my own city neighborhood, across the same distance I am walking now, I pass at least twenty houses, along a single block. I love the diversity of beautiful humanity in the city, but I am also drawn to the peace and anonymity this open landscape affords.

One evening in early autumn, having escaped the bustle inside, I walk alone down the gravel road just before sunset, slowly sauntering north down the half mile leading to the stop sign. Except for an occasional car passing on the blacktop road ahead, I am completely alone, accompanied merely by the noise of chirping crickets, lightly cooing birds, and the wind sending dust across my ankles.

To my left, the sun has already begun its descent toward the earth. It's much closer and fuller this evening, hovering just above the tree-line, low and round like a giant orange plucked from a Cézanne painting. The waning light is soft enough that I can observe the scene for a few seconds without burning my eyes, but bright enough that I must look away often, glancing back at the dirt beneath my feet. The memory of round light lingers in tiny spheres, flashing across my eyes with each blink.

Because I'm focused on the sun, it takes a moment for me to shift my gaze, to remember that the horizon is all around me. But when I finally turn my head to the right, just far enough, I catch a surprise in my peripheral vision—another large, round sphere in gentle orange, the sun's waning light written across its cratered face.

Sunset and moonrise, together.

On both sides of me, earth's two celestial bodies balance, like a scale in which I am the fulcrum, except I have no role but mere witness. They seem to be facing off, perhaps teasing one another—the light from the sun illuminating the moon, the moon tossing back the same light, playfully exchanging night and day. Although they are both desperately far from where I am walking on the spinning earth, they might as well be pies from the dessert table, waiting for me to reach out and take a slice. I stop walking and stand there on the road between them.

Beauty is often surprising, appearing when one isn't looking. Of course, in one sense this scene is not surprising at all; if I paid closer attention to the lunar phases, I could have predicted and planned to be here on this very night. Instead, while searching for something else, merely a quiet moment, I wandered right into the middle of it all. A weary, young mom trying to momentarily escape the demands of her life on an unnamed dirt road, is suddenly bookended by two great lights.

In Marilynne Robinson's masterpiece *Gilead*, a young John Ames describes a journey to Kansas alongside his father, searching for his grandfather's grave—a long and difficult quest, finally rewarded in an overgrown graveyard in rural Kansas. After cleaning up the gravestone, young Ames's father bows his head to offer a prayer. There, in the middle of that forlorn graveyard, in the middle of a long prayer, Ames looks up to the same scene I am witnessing now—the sun setting as the moon rises on a wide horizon. "I would never have thought this place could be beautiful," Ames's father utters in response.

A place like Kansas rewards the quiet search—the journey of one who is not entirely sure what they are looking for, or even if they will find it. I have come searching for this farm road many times, if only to arrive on time for holiday dinner or take a deeper breath. I have never come searching like a tourist following directions to a famous place, camera in hand, waiting for a photo shoot. Walking out here alone, I do not have a way to take a picture. Even if I did, I couldn't capture the whole horizon in its frame.

On that lonely farm road between the sun and the moon, I am overcome again by the vastness of the sky and horizon. I do not know where to look. The horizon is too big, the scene too wonderful for my scope of vision. I keep turning my head, looking to the left, then to the right, then left and right again, west and east, back and forth, as if my head is on a swivel. I try to turn toward the beauty, but it's all around me. Like most deeply sacred things, this is not a beauty my human eyesight is able to fully take in.

So until the spinning earth sends us all out of balance—the sun lowering, the moon becoming smaller as it rises in the sky—I simply stand on the hidden farm road and experience the joy of having gone searching, and somehow being found.

Bats and Bees (and Mice and Wasps)

On creature wrestling

"Like Jacob's angel, the region requires that you wrestle with it before it bestows a blessing."
–Kathleen Norris, *Dakota*

When Kathleen Norris says the plains require wrestling before blessing, I know her meaning is broader than battling against the landscape's smallest creatures. Still, some of my own wrestling matches have been of the micro sort—long summer days nursing my itchy mosquito bites, finding tiny bumps across my sandaled feet from chiggers, or submitting to my mother's dutiful checks for ticks in my hair. Once, she burned out a large tick with the end of a hot match, coaxing it to move from its lodging place just above my ear. These small creatures find their way into cracks and crevices, hiding themselves inside our lives and homes and stories. I often wonder if there is any way to win this sort of wrestling—to bless or receive a blessing from these small, unwelcome creatures.

Brad's family once rented a rural home several miles north of tiny Luray, Kansas, in Russell County. They only lived there for six months, as a transitional window before moving a bit farther east for another job. But when that house and time come up, his family always mentions the loveliness of the property, the house nestled in a valley surrounded by hills and towering oaks. Driving there was welcoming, they say, and the boys loved scattering and playing on the surrounding property and exploring the nearby creek.

But after they describe the place, the conversation quickly turns to the bees. That little house was infested with a whole hive of bees taking up residence in the walls and ceiling. Brad remembers fighting off the stinging insects outside as he played, and his mom recounts how bees often chased his Grandpa Sonny when he came over to work on the property, forcing him to seek shelter inside.

There were so many bees, and clearly also a honeycomb, that honey would sometimes seep down from the ceiling and into a light fixture.

"I just put a piece of bread up there," my father-in-law jokes.

As if the bee infestation were not enough, bats also found their way into the basement and attic. Once, while Brad's dad was away, a bat emerged inside. Brad and his two brothers donned their "bat gear"—blankets and stocking hats—and ran around waving brooms, saving the day by swatting that bat out of the house and somehow avoiding any bites. And yet, they still talk about that home with fondness, their battles with the bats and bees sounding nearly like an epic, one of gooey sweetness dripping down into the light.

One weekend in late summer, Brad and I book an overnight stay at a country home while the kids are with my parents. We stay in a small blue house once owned by a family's beloved grandmother, the property now converted into a guest house for others to enjoy. I already know from perusing the woman's still intact bookcase that I would have loved chatting with her, as her shelves are lined with *The Great Gatsby*, *Wuthering Heights*, authors like Bill Bryson and Madeleine L'Engle, plus several books on Kansas history. Soon after we arrive, I sit at an upright vintage Vose & Sons piano and pluck hymns out of a songbook while light falls across the floor and Brad sprawls on the couch with a book.

These early hours have the makings of a peaceful twenty-four hours away in rural Kansas. But later, as I am working in the kitchen, I find tiny black spots dotted across the blue counters.

I inhale. It's the country, I remind myself, sweeping up the droppings and sanitizing as best as I can, hoping they are remains of mice long gone. Still, we decide to put out traps, just in case. We find a trap in the pantry, load it, and set it behind a kitchen cabinet.

My own beloved Grandma Jessie used to collect mice, or at least images of them, sewn onto hand towels or painted onto platters. Decorative mice always remind me of her kitchen, a place full of wonderful childhood memories against a backdrop of collectible field mice, their eyes round, sweet, and innocent. Fictional mice like Stuart Little or those found in Kate DiCamillo's books are charming too, but I do not know if real mice can ever be blessed.

The next morning, I find Brad not downstairs in the living room, relaxing on the couch where I expect him, but tucked into a small bedroom lined with lace curtains on the second floor. "I'm avoiding the mice," he mutters, then reports how that morning as he went to make his coffee, a mouse emerged and sprinted across the living room, with the trap still attached to one of its hind legs. As the mouse scurried away, it dragged the trap along behind (I do feel a bit bad about this detail of the story) and slipped into the narrow space just behind the piano.

"It's still back there," Brad half whispers from his perch on the bed. Clearly, he has donned no "mice gear" to protect us from this critter. Instead, we hastily stack our luggage onto tables and remain upstairs for the duration of our stay, hiding from that tiny, injured mouse, just as it hides behind the piano from us.

On another weekend away for our anniversary, Brad and I stay at a barn that has been converted into an apartment, located on a cattle farm in south central Kansas. The owner, who I'll call Sharon, is a kind soul, great storyteller, and hearty cook, who brings us fresh bread every morning and chats with us on the back patio at night as stars emerge from their cocoons and crickets sing into the balminess of summer.

"If you want to explore the place," Sharon tells me, "You're free to cross the creek and walk out into the pasture. You just need to open the gate," she says, pointing out a cluster of trees down the hill. "And make sure you get it shut so the animals don't get out." She proceeds to tell a story of waking up one morning to discover the entire entrance to the farm filled with cattle.

The next morning, while Brad is inside reading, I decide I'm going on a walk into the pasture with the cattle, just as Sharon has shown me. I ready myself for the excursion by rehearsing her instructions to be particularly mindful of the gate.

I hike down a narrow path until I reach the creek bed. I haven't packed the best hiking shoes, but I climb through the shin-deep grasses anyway, imagining the joy of this romp through the prairie, and how I'll brag to Brad about everything he missed.

But as I reach out and unlock the gate, a cluster of insects, including at least three or four wasps, swirls up in a hungry swarm. I take a half-step backwards, instinctively flapping my arms around my body. A sharp, incisive pain radiates from the center of my left arm. Meanwhile, other wasps continue to rotate, clearly angry I have disturbed them.

I turn and take off full speed, running back up the path toward the barn. At least one wasp still follows, so I wildly wave my arms behind me—a scene for all the farmhands to enjoy.

I have dreamt of spending my afternoon wandering across the prairie, exploring the gifts of a generous, spacious landscape. But I suppose I have not been tenacious enough to receive today's blessing. My wrestling match ends on the couch inside the converted barn, where Sharon brings me an ice pack for my throbbing arm.

Keys from My Grandma

On gifts given and received

"Whatever we have been given is supposed to be given away again . . ."
—Lewis Hyde, *The Gift*

My eight-year-old frame is perched on a thin, rickety metal barstool in Grandma Jessie's kitchen. Grandma Jessie leans forward onto the yellow countertops, a shade lighter than creamy Dijon mustard, and begins answering the questions I have just posed for a school assignment.

What was it like to be born during the Depression?

Where did you live?

What did you do for fun?

She describes her dad working in Oklahoma oil fields and moving the family around often for his work. She talks about attending different grade schools and living without many "extras." She explains how she eventually moved to the small town of Haven, Kansas, where she met Grandpa Don, got married at age nineteen, and raised three children.

I inscribe her answers onto my notebook paper, slowly and diligently, in the same way I have been writing in my very first diary, which Grandma Jessie gave me for my eighth birthday. Covered in autumn-colored flowers, each page is lined with golden edges and sealed from the outside world with a lock and key. Whenever I want to write my secret thoughts, I place the tiny key inside the lock and twist it open, then turn the key again to tuck those stories away.

For the same birthday, Grandma Jessie gifted me another special set of keys—her old, electric Sears typewriter. We did not have a computer at our house then, so the typewriter was my first keyboard. Grandma Jessie showed me how to plug in the machine, carefully load a sheet of white computer paper, and click the keys while the electric carriage moved across the page.

Grandma Jessie worked at an insurance agency after high school where she had become a master typist. I watched her fingers fly across those keys, creating words faster than I had ever seen anyone make them before.

My own attempts were clumsy, resulting in frequent pauses to load the white-out correction paper. Grandma Jessie showed me how to back the typewriter up one space, strike the exact same key again, and see the mistaken letter disappear behind a powdery, white glaze.

Even at a young age, I understood Grandma Jessie was giving me something wonderful in this little exchange—offering me pieces of her own story and keys to begin writing my own.

I am a little older, maybe in late elementary school, when I sit down beside Grandma Jessie and peek over her shoulder to see what she is doing. She is holding a half-folded newspaper in one hand and a yellow pencil in the other. Through her reading glasses, she peers closely at a word puzzle called cryptoquip. I stay beside her and watch as she takes only one clue (Q = A) and begins working to decode some mysterious message.

"Well, what do you think?" Grandma Jessie never looks up, but she honors my presence by muttering her thoughts aloud as she works.

"This three-letter word could be 'the,' maybe?" She sketches it in with her pencil, adds a few letters elsewhere, then immediately erases them.

"No, it's 'for,' I think. See, you know because the 'th' combination isn't showing up anywhere else."

I feel as though I am watching her fingers move across those typewriter keys again—this is something I want to learn, too.

After Grandma Jessie solves the cryptoquip, she moves on to the jumble. Unscrambling letters makes more sense to me. Still, before I have even unscrambled the shorter words, she has already solved the final jumble, as though the whole process is not difficult at all.

I begin helping Grandma Jessie with the newspaper word games whenever I am at her house. I practice them on my own, too, slowly understanding how these puzzles work, growing in my confidence that I can solve them. It feels like holding a small golden key and turning it inside a lock.

"I tell you, this is too fancy for me," Grandma Jessie says, flustered.

In the summer of 2020, Grandma Jessie is using her first iPhone, which we had delivered to her assisted living center. The process of getting her to answer the phone has been—well, a process. It has taken about thirty minutes of calling back and forth with no answer—plus my mom phoning her landline a few times to tell her we were trying to call—and finally, one of the facility workers showing up to help. But now, across the screen, we can see her face.

Seeing Grandma Jessie's face right now is no small thing. She has been inside her assisted living center and has not left the building, even for a small errand, in months.

"I'm still used to the ol' party lines," Grandma Jessie goes on. "If the person ahead of you wasn't finished, you'd just listen to their conversation."

I balance my phone in one hand while a squirming child sits on my lap. As Grandma Jessie talks, I picture myself back in her kitchen at age eight, diligently taking notes. I cannot remember everything she told me then, but I am determined not to forget what she is telling me now, nearly thirty years later.

"And these new computers, I tell you!" she says. "We had those old typewriters."

"Yeah, Grandma, you gave me your old electric one when I was a kid," I say. "Do you remember?"

She stops and looks at me for a moment.

"No," she says, shaking her head slightly. "I guess I don't remember."

Grandma Jessie, in her mid-eighties now, is quite active. But she no longer types or uses the computer, and it has been years since we have done a cryptoquip together. I find myself listening extra closely to her stories during these pandemic days. I am afraid to forget anything she has taught me, everything she has lived and knows. I feel an increasing pull to not only tuck away all these stories, both mine and my family's, but also to draw them out and learn to unlock them.

When it is safer to travel, we drive the four hours from Kansas City to Hutchinson and visit Grandma Jessie. Last year, around this time, I came to see her and found her wearing a cowboy hat, doing a dance challenge with her senior exercise class. But the pandemic has slowed things down. Her group activities have been more limited. She eats lunch in a small group and has designated times to go outside. At this point, she also cannot have any visitors in the building. Instead, once a week, she can see someone by talking to them on a phone through a window.

The bench for our window visit is set up inside a bed of gravel rocks with no shade from the building. It is 3:00 PM in mid-August, and with no cloud cover, the heat is oppressive. When we arrive, Grandma Jessie is already sitting on the other side of the glass, smiling and waving, holding a flip phone.

I talk to her on speakerphone from the other side of the window, trying to draw out little pieces of her story.

How is the food?

How are you spending your time?

Did you watch the baseball game last night?

As we talk, my son plays with rocks, and my daughter colors quietly in a coloring book. The kids stop to answer questions and tell her stories, but it is hard for them to pay attention to a conversation that is happening through a wall. I wonder what stories they will remember from these days, or what they will remember about their great grandma.

Even with the heat and restrictions, it is wonderful to see Grandma Jessie. When we leave thirty minutes later, she cries, like she always has throughout the years whenever anyone leaves.

After I am back in the car, I cry too. I am deeply grateful she is safe and healthy, but I grieve that the same window that keeps the virus out also keeps Grandma Jessie inside. It feels like we are all living inside a very complicated puzzle, with no easy answer to help us move forward.

I carry this tension back to my parents' house where we are staying. In the kitchen, the local newspaper is sitting on the counter, as it often is—a detail I find comforting. Later that night, I flip to the word game section and find a fresh cryptoquip waiting for me, with one solitary clue: T equals W

It always feels daunting, that little exchange of letters—only one tiny clue to unlock the whole message. But I remember all the times Grandma Jessie and I played this game together, her yellow pencil moving around the newspaper as quickly as her fingers across a typewriter.

I pick up my pencil, this one simple motion that can unlock a hidden story. When everything feels uncertain, here's something small I can do—arrange letters and form them into words. Grandma Jessie has handed me the key.

Scenic Overlook

On seeking healing

". . . I asked what was so special about the Flint Hills. Picking and handling her words carefully as if they were newborn, taking her time, she said, *These hills are so everlasting.*"
—William Least Heat-Moon, *PrairyErth*

The prairie is a sort of ocean. Of course, this is the kind of claim a person makes only if they grew up six hundred miles away from the nearest coastline. Surely people who live on the edge of the sea, listening to the ongoing roar of the waves, would dispute the notion. But if an ocean is a place where you can stand at the edge of an expanse far larger than yourself and watch it extend all the way to the line of the horizon, then the Great Plains, a swath of earth covering over a million square miles, where the wind blows grass into constant motion, feels oceanic to me.

One afternoon, in the spring of 2021, I stand on the side of I-35 at mile marker 111: the Bazaar Cattle Pens scenic overlook. When we passed the sign announcing the overlook minutes ago, I made an impulsive decision to slow the minivan and pull over. At that point, I was only one hour into the nearly four-hour drive from Kansas City to Hutchinson, alone with my five-year-old daughter in the back seat.

As I clicked my blinker and steered toward the exit, my daughter asked what we were doing.

"I just want to stop and look for a minute," I told her, assuring her we would not delay our trip to see her grandparents any longer than necessary. She whined about the detour, but I persisted. I have passed this overlook dozens of times and stopped maybe once before. I am too often in a hurry, zooming by at seventy-five miles per hour, determined to make it to my destination.

But right now, I have nowhere else to be. The Kansas landscape and open sky are the reasons I came.

After parking, unbuckling, and unloading, my daughter and I lean against the railing on the interstate overpass, alongside a few other travelers who have stopped, too. Ahead of us, the Flint Hills stretch out their arms. The limestone and shale outcrops, and the shadows created by their texture, do resemble cresting waves, rising and falling under a sky of scattered clouds. The curving lines of each hill are covered in newly green prairie grasses, vibrant after recent prescribed burning, a practice that farmers participate in each year to keep the land healthy. As those fires have snaked their way across pastureland, they have burned away invasive shrubs and trees that would otherwise overtake everything—a key to this land's resilience. The burning prevents further wildfires and releases nutrients into the ground, creating healthier conditions for the grazing cattle, which roam along the ledges. Although I cannot see them now, a herd of antelope has been reintroduced to this area and can sometimes be spotted in the distance.

As we stand on the gravel and take in the view, the Kansas wind snaps at my shirt and tosses hair and dust across my face. Cars continue passing on the interstate, our detour placing us far behind fellow travelers who carry on at high speeds. After only a few minutes, my daughter begins to squirm against my legs, ready to get back on the road.

I know the feeling, I think.

I, too, love having a destination—somewhere I'm trying to arrive. In that sense, I can understand why so many travelers grumble about having to cross Kansas on their way to the mountains, lamenting all those hours it takes to reach your destination.

But today, I am not rushing forward. I'm trying to stay present to my life.

I am here to be.

———

Earlier in the week, from across a Zoom screen, my therapist and I made a list—a to-do list, of sorts. The list included simple, daily things, like attending my kids' activities and practices, sitting outside in the spring evening air with other moms, passing time, chatting, and snacking. It included spending as much time with Brad as possible, falling asleep each night by placing my ear against his chest and matching the cadence of his breath. It instructed me to eat food I loved and chew slowly, savoring each bite. (Egg, bacon, and jam biscuits from a favorite Kansas City coffee shop were at the top of the list.)

Also on the list—drive home to Kansas. Kansas is only ten minutes away from my current home, just across the state line, but I understood this meant back to central Kansas, into the big-sky, wheatfield part of Kansas, placing myself as much as possible between the seam of wide earth and open sky. While there, I also hoped to visit family members who loved me simply for being me, without any expectation to be or do anything spectacular.

It was a strange sort of assignment for someone who had spent years of her life making to-do lists in the service of productivity. But these are the kind of lists you must make when, after weeks of not sleeping, you find that the hope you once had for the future has suddenly dwindled and darkened. It's what happens when you open your eyes one morning and feel unable to get out of bed to take the kids to school.

I made it through the first year of the pandemic thinking I was doing okay, or at least that's what I kept saying. But in the spring, just as businesses and schools in our area began opening back up, my mind began shutting down. I suppose I can blame it on the usual suspects of those unprecedented times: too many days on end in my house overseeing virtual school, several deaths in our family, cultural division, the harrowing corners of the internet, fractures in our institutions, even local ones like church, school, and community. Those were days of grief upon grief; change stacked upon change.

What is a person to do when the changes finally stack up so high that it feels they will topple you, when it feels daunting to imagine any way forward?

I began driving back home to Kansas.

"Like a replicating virus, all despair can make is more of itself," writes John Green in *The Anthropocene Reviewed*, a book borne out of the pandemic days. Indeed, my own despair had been replicating inside the four walls of my home, spreading like an invasive weed, quickly growing out of control. Much like Green describes of his disorienting experience as a student hospital chaplain, we had all witnessed senseless suffering during the pandemic, and my brain struggled to make meaning. I didn't want to walk away from things I held dear: faith, hope, community, a sense of purpose. But I couldn't easily access the anchors I once found steadying.

So perhaps it was a counter impulse that compelled me back to the Kansas landscape. If despair and anxiety were threatening to overtake me, could I find something even bigger and more expansive than despair? When my mind was struggling to hold faith in a larger story beyond me, could I at least move my body into a more expansive space?

Nine months earlier, when stay-at-home orders first lifted, we had gone to central Kansas to see my parents for the first time since the pandemic began. Although I was in better mental shape then, we had already been at home for months, piled on top of each other with our computers and virtual learning. While there, Brad and I were able to have a short date night. We drove twenty minutes from Hutchinson to

Yoder, Kansas, a small, Amish Mennonite community with a restaurant called Carriage Crossing where our family had often gathered for birthdays or a slice of coffee cake. We ordered takeout, then drove down K-96 toward my late Grandpa Don's farm.

That night smelled like lemony grilled cod with a side of syrupy sweet potatoes, cinnamon-buttered rolls, and a piece of chocolate pie, all consumed eagerly in the passenger seat out of a Styrofoam container. We drove on county roads past the stubble of just-harvested wheatfields, breathing in wide swaths of ground and uninterrupted conversation after months of feeling squeezed.

Finally, we parked outside the gate of my grandpa's farm and hiked into the overgrown pasture. It had been a rainy spring, so the pond was completely full—a rare sight, some years—and the grass was tall enough to tickle my knees and hide the sheep poop that smeared the bottom of my slip-on shoes as I walked.

As sunset turned the edges of the horizon coral and a half-moon appeared, I stood by the edge of the pond and watched cars ticking past on the highway while the sun settled behind low lines of crop-protecting trees. The wind's steady gusts sent the surface of the pond into narrow ripples of reflected sky.

After all those days at home, although I was merely standing in a sheep-poop covered pasture next to a tiny pond—big enough for only a canoe or a pedal boat—I breathed deeply for the first time in months. Experts say that simply being near a large body of water, like the ocean, calms anxiety. But here in the middle of the prairie, by this simple pond and expansive sky, I might as well have been standing on the edge of the ocean.

Green writes that he loves his home of Indianapolis "precisely because it isn't easy to love." There has never been a more Midwestern sentiment, and I would argue that it's even truer of growing up in Kansas, spending your formative years laughing off all those "there's no place like home" and "you're not in Kansas anymore" references.

Kansas is not always easy to love, but I love the landscape because it endures all sorts of harsh weather conditions—golf ball-sized hail, drought, fierce winds, tornadoes, sweltering heat, bitter cold—yet it retains the tenacious sort of tenderness that is required to grow things.

The landscape suffers, but it also persists. Some of the land's suffering is simply a result of its location in the middle of the Great Plains, where the southern gulf air and western mountain air collide and form into extreme weather. But some of it is a forced tenacity, designed to help the land come back stronger and full of more growth than before. These Flint Hills are not green all year, like grass planted in wetter climates. The grass fades to brown during the dryer months of winter, then withers and disappears entirely as the earth is scorched black during the burning season, when patches of dark earth line the highway. If you drive by a field just after it is burned, you could be tempted to think life is long gone. But within weeks, new sprouts appear—the whole scene changed.

When I leave the scenic overlook and return to the minivan, re-buckling my daughter and pulling back onto the interstate, despair is still a heavy cloak riding along beside me. Human healing does not always match the seasons, and my own scorched-earth tenderness will not throttle into green shoots nearly as quickly as on the hills. Still, there has been a sort of hope in the act of returning, in standing near these expansive waves of the prairie, these tides that endure.

Mile Markers

On finding a way forward

"As they pass through the Valley of Baca,
They make it a spring"
—Psalm 84:6

Let the rest of the world fall away, with its dreams, plans, and visions for the future. Let the endless news scroll across the thumbs of another. All you can—must—do today is hold the wheel steady, let the pale green earth pass you by, each mile marker keeping steady time—another minute you have found the courage to go on.

Beyond the window, flattened ground stretches a wide embrace; electrical poles quietly carry light; the sky, unburdened by clouds, smiles blue. But you are seeking cover from the storm brewing inside, from your rotating thoughts, a turbulence you cannot yet name.

At home, your days have passed in seemingly normal endeavors. You haul trash to the curb, wave politely at the neighbors, check the bill-ridden mail. You pick up after the children, sweep crumbs from the counter, unload another round of dishes. You catch up on doctor appointments after a year of closures, trying to calm your children as the dentist works on the handful of cavities eating away at their baby teeth, a casualty of the office closing for yet another virus exposure, plus a tired mother who kept forgetting to reschedule new appointments. *Mea culpa*, kids.

Each morning, you slide on your yoga pants, one leg and chipped-toenail-polish-foot at a time, stumble downstairs, and start the kettle for tea. Tea, of all things. The loss of your morning coffee felt like the final loss in a year full of losses, the one steady routine you were still holding in your clenched fist. But on that Tuesday afternoon when you hid inside your closet and described your symptoms to a doctor over the phone, trying to ignore the children yelling loudly in the hallway, she prescribed a caffeine-less existence before anything else. "Caffeine causes anxiety," she said. And although you were fairly confident not drinking caffeine would also cause anxiety, you did what you must, what it turns out you must always do in these moments—you surrendered. You released your hold on that mug of pressed beans, trading them for dried mushrooms and chicory root teas, sorry substitutes though they are.

Without coffee, you must embrace other small joys. You take your kid out to lunch on a Thursday since he is still in school part-time because of the virus, and you watch the young skin around his eyes crinkle as he takes another bite of chips and salsa. You look into those eyes and remind yourself this is why you will keep showing up, one caffeine-less day after another. You cannot hold the fracturing world together, but you can hold these two humans who call you mother in your arms, letting their youth and hope buoy you.

You watch every baseball practice perched on the grassy hill just above home plate, making small talk with the other moms. You have always hated small talk, but now you need anything, everything, packaged in small and light and easy. Thank God for small talk. Baseball cleat brands, the weather, what Junior ate for breakfast. When practice is over, you gather up all the items scattered around the hill and pack everyone up for home, the kids begging for snacks and insisting they need another meal before bedtime.

You, too, focus on eating. One afternoon, your friend Sandee brings you lunch—actually, she brings four lunches—and you sit outside on the porch while your daughter spins about in ballet performances and chew a deli sandwich slathered with bacon and dill mayo and avocado, immersing yourself in the flavors, the texture. You eat the leftovers for the next three days and feel relieved your friend brought you far more than you knew you needed, because you needed all of it, every last crunch alongside every in-person word and gesture of friendship, after months with too much isolation.

And on the weekends, whenever you can, you drive. Through the six traffic lights that always seem to turn red as you arrive, onto the highway exit, up on the interstate, out of the city, until you are under a canopy of sky. How many drives do you make to central Kansas that spring? A half dozen maybe, alone or with your family, each journey a confession, *mea culpa*, for the exhaust you are sending into the air, *mea culpa*, that you could not have held steadier under the pressure cooker of the year, that you could not have been a social media warrior valiantly fighting misinformation with your thumbs because you could not even valiantly fight off the daily stack of dishes.

Here, under the sky, the road widens into four lanes, green signs tick off each interval, simple farms and windmills and tree rows pass softly, almost without notice. You try to ignore the string of billboards, lacking the energy to rage or even sigh at the ways they shout for you to invest in real estate or vote in elections that have long-since been decided. You cannot even traverse this landscape without reminders of how divided we are, how divided you feel within yourself. This is your Valley of Baca, a place you have called home, now turned wilderness.

You must pass through.

Wilderness, Kosuke Koyama wrote in *Three Mile an Hour God*, is an "open space in all directions . . . full of promise and full of danger." You sense the danger, right here with you. But what about the promise? Where is it now?

The road narrows again as the land gathers up into hills, shadows lingering inside their folds while drops of inky cattle cluster around shallow ponds. The lanes gently sweep you back and forth, rocking you toward your own starting place. You are no longer quite sure if you are coming or going, if you belong here or no longer belong, but you know you must return, again.

Soon, the road flattens out and the exit signs become familiar, as old as your memories. You work your way back like a salmon in a minivan, swimming home. Across a smaller road to divert around the city traffic, past that familiar exit where cars often line up, nose to nose, then you are back on K-96, this highway you drove so many times in childhood. You will not honk as you pass the old cottonwood tree, for you are too weary for celebration or even luck, today. Instead, you round the curve methodically, like someone whose very muscle memory holds these routes.

And once you are over the flat earth, at your parents' house or the house along the old farm road, you finally rest. In months when sleep has been fitful and halting, this is a gift—the ability to slip into the night for a few hours rather than staring into looming darkness, fighting back the fearful edges.

One morning in late May, when the wheat is still green but glowing with the faintest of gold, you wake up on the farm and squint at the clock. It's still in the five o'clock hour, far too early to be awake. But the light is already lining the edge of the blinds, and through them, you see a sliver of pink, a slip of color. A nudge. Come and see.

Almost nothing will get you out of bed faster than the promise of a Kansas sunrise. In these days when getting out of bed has been achingly slow, you feel nearly surprised at the speed your body finds itself upright. You push your legs onto the floor and stick your nose inside the blinds, the quarter inch between its panels telling you all you need to know. In the words of Louisiana Elefante's teacher in Kate DiCamillo's *Louisiana's Way Home*, the earth is constantly moving, rotating in endless motion, "infinitesimally." But when you watch the sunrise it does not feel infinitesimal. At these seams of the day, you can sense exactly how fast you are spinning, you know how quickly the sun will pop above the horizon and spread the air bright with refracted light. What is the opposite of infinitesimal? That is how fast you must now move if you are to witness it. You pull on a shirt over your leggings and slide into your sandals. You trip over the edge of a suitcase and swallow a yelp, hoping you have not woken anyone.

Outside, outside, past the trees, where the birds and crickets are already awake, singing to each other in wild orchestra. Your sandals find the dirt road and suddenly, nothing is between you and the sky but a distant line of trees marking off another square of farmland, and that sky is now upon you, over you, around you—a metamorphosis of color after the harrowing cocoon of night. Yesterday, this was an ordinary field, these were merely green wheat stalks flopping gently in the breeze, slowly ripening into yellow. Now, a swirl of gold splashes above the tree line, shooting light pillars as high as it can, while the background of the sky, the whole maddening expanse of Kansas sky, has turned purple, and the clouds are searing pink, the color of your daughter's joy. The morning is shouting hope, but not shouting like the billboards—no, this sky is exuberant but calm, a mother who has witnessed the five-year-old, twelve-year-old, thirty-something-year-old versions of you who have stood beneath its expanse.

So many places in the world are stunning in their own right; you don't know it yet, but not many years from now, you will have seen some of the grandest views in the world—Lake Como, the Cliffs of Moher, the north shore of Mallorca. No one questions the beauty of those places, where travelers flock and write raving reviews on travel blogs, where the expanse of blue ocean crashes against cliffs, where distended mountains rise from a creamy green earth.

But the image you will carry around—inside of you, on your six-inch phone screen, eventually printed and propped by your bedside thousands of miles from home, is from that desperate pilgrimage in May when you remembered that surprise can be hidden in a quiet, landlocked field, when you witnessed the flat earth bubbling up, frothing over, becoming a spring.

Leaving at Intermission

On not knowing

"... the place our mothers and fathers
and theirs and theirs passed through ..."
—Wyatt Townley, "Centering the House"

The afternoon sky near Bazaar, Kansas, unfolds in layers of blue—color scattering more lightly at the horizon, slowly giving way to a richer, more potent blue overhead. Puffs of clouds casually hang in midair, but they draw no attention to themselves. They also obscure none of the sun's rays in today's ninety-degree heat.

I emerge onto the Flint Hills landscape alongside my mom, stepping out of her car into a large makeshift parking lot on the edge of a field. Hundreds of other cars have arrived here ahead of us, now arranged in long, messy lines. We stretch our arms after driving from my parents' house in Hutchinson, then begin loading ourselves up like modern-day pack mules—sunglasses, sunscreen, water bottles, snacks, blankets (only for sitting on, in this weather), bug spray, folding chairs. Both of us pull floppy-brimmed hats over our heads, feeling ridiculous but knowing this may be the only shade we will see until dusk.

We have come for the 2022 Symphony in the Flint Hills, a yearly event in which the Kansas City Symphony plays under a tented orchestral shell in the middle of a field. Thousands of people descend upon the prairie to hear classical music against the backdrop of prairie grasses, cattle, and endless sky.

I have heard the Kansas City Symphony perform several times at its usual home, the Kauffman Center for the Performing Arts. There, you can stand in a climate-controlled lobby near a giant wall of windows, sipping a drink while looking across a twinkly downtown skyline. You can nestle yourself into a plush chair in a wood-paneled auditorium designed to offer concertgoers the right blend of comfort and acoustics.

But I am most eager to hear the symphony out here, beneath the sky and setting sun. In all my years living in the Midwest, this is my first time attending the event. Many summers, I have looked longingly at photos, wishing to join if only our summer travel had landed differently, or if tickets weren't so hard to come by. But now, the dirt of this temporary parking lot is beneath my two feet, sweat is seeping down my hairline, and my own shoulder is weighed down by bags and folding chairs. I am here—and still surprised about it. This wasn't exactly the plan.

Just yesterday, Brad and I were eating breakfast at the Clover Cliff Ranch near Elmdale, enjoying a spread of eggs and bacon in the limestone main house. It was the last morning of our stay at the ranch, positioned on the edge of a bison-lined pasture. We had come to celebrate our anniversary while the kids stayed with their grandparents—a brief parenting respite. In the evenings, we wandered out on the gravel pathway to the limestone fence with its circular archway and watched the sun nestle behind the hills. During the day, we crawled out into the field, dodging mud and thistles and spotting a few small lizards in the rocky earth. With the owner's permission, we even crossed the little valley separating the main property from the bison pasture and stepped out into the bison's grazing land, keeping a safe distance from the animals but feeling the joy and vulnerability of sharing space with such powerful living creatures who are native to the region.

As our trip drew to a close, I was eager to see the kids again, but I also ate my breakfast with a side of longing, wishing I could stay in these hills and open spaces a bit longer. Around that time, Susie, one of the owners of the ranch, came by our table to offer us a refill on drinks. She mentioned she had two extra tickets to the next day's Symphony in the Flint Hills.

"Would you be interested?" she asked. "I would hate for them to go to waste."

I gasped, ready to accept. Then I caught Brad's eye, which seemed a bit less eager. "We would love that, but of course we need to check with our parents about the kids," I replied, already plotting how we could make the logistics work. Susie said she understood, and as she walked away, Brad pulled out his phone to check the weather forecast.

"It's gonna be too hot," he said, after a quick scroll to see temperatures in the 90s with full sun. "I'm out."

Later, I will discover his instant compulsion to check the weather has fallen right in line with this year's symphony theme, "Weather in the Flint Hills." Just a week before the event, Dave Kendall, longtime event emcee, posed an inquiry in the *Kansas Reflector*: "Will the weather cooperate?"

Will it cooperate? I imagine the Kansas weather joining the event planning committee and sitting through meetings nodding its head, agreeing to deliver a perfect June day while secretly crossing two fingers behind its back.

The show has carried on in all kinds of conditions, shutting down only once for extreme weather in 2019 and for the pandemic in 2020. In the same article in the *Reflector*, Kendall quotes event organizer Emily Hunter who says the event is not for everyone. "At its heart," she says, the experience is "an adventure."

Susie returned to the table a few minutes later, asking again what we thought and if she should offer the tickets to someone else. Dismissing my husband as a fair-weather symphony-goer, I accepted the tickets and offered the extra spot to my mom. She agreed right away.

On site for the symphony, our adventure begins as soon as we adjust our loads and leave the parking lot. There are only two ways to get to the concert location in the field: we could wait in a long line for a carriage ride in a Conestoga wagon or walk the meandering trail ourselves.

Mom and I look at each other from behind our sunglasses, the bill of our hats drooping in our eyes.

"What do you think?" I ask. My legs are thirty years younger than hers, but she walks the neighborhood almost daily, staying in better shape.

We eye the line for the wagon ride. We walk up to the wagons until we are nearly in the queue, but we hover for a moment, assessing the line's length and considering how long we could be waiting. An hour, maybe more. To our left, a narrow dirt path scrawls across the grassy hills, dotted with a string of other concertgoers who have chosen the footpath. In the distance, the tips of white tents poke up from the folds of the hills—our destination just within sight.

"I think we can walk it," I say.

My mom hesitates. I wonder if she is having flashbacks to the time I convinced her, during my first year of teaching, to take a spring break trip to New York City. Neither of us had ever been to the Big Apple, and I wanted to see everything, but without looking too much like a tourist. I dragged us all over the city, insisting we should not over-consult our maps or our phones, which meant we walked even more steps than needed.

We stood on the Empire State Building, waited outside the TODAY show filming with signs ("Mom and Daughter teachers from Kansas [heart] New York"), wandered through Central Park, and attended a showing of Lin-Manuel Miranda's *In the Heights*. When our flight home from LaGuardia was canceled due to weather, we rebooked a flight across the state line in New Jersey and caught a train to stay with one of my college friends living in the area. The train stalled at multiple points because of the storm, and we slept on my friend's couch for only two hours before catching our new flight home, returning exhausted.

But now, after a short pause, my mom simply shrugs her shoulders. "I'm with you," she says.

We veer left, setting off on the path through the hills.

The thing about "Weather in the Flint Hills," or weather in any region of Kansas, is that it offers an ongoing answer to those who dismiss the landscape as boring. "Watch this," it says, switching hour to hour, day to day, rolling through seasons and sometimes seasons within seasons like a teenager changing clothes before an event.

Even the *Travel Kansas* website warns visitors about the weather's "significant variability," a polite way to say that the weather is moody, constantly changing, upending things, happy to surprise. Meteorologists can accurately predict patterns, of course, understanding the science of how conditions are created and giving us a sense of what's coming, often saving lives in the process. But anyone who watches the weather report over even a few days knows that meteorologists are not omniscient.

We make plans; the weather changes them. We walk toward things, thinking we have an idea of where we are headed, but we never know exactly what we will find on the other side. When it comes to Kansas weather, perhaps Shakespeare said it best in *As You Like It*—we are "merely players" on this landscape.

Only a few hundred feet into our walk toward the symphony site, my armpits begin leaking through my deodorant barrier. My bag and the folding chair I'm carrying chafe against my shoulder as my breath begins to come more rapidly. We are carrying a dozen pounds of weight each, at least, and we're also pulling hills. Shallow prairie hills, maybe, but still a hearty incline. Every few minutes, we crest another ridge, and I can see the large white canopy floating out in the field with clusters of people already milling about. Then, we dip back into a valley and lose our line of sight.

Even with our combined years living in the Midwest, my mom and I seem to have forgotten a simple truth—objects on the prairie landscape are much farther away than they appear.

About halfway through, my mom looks at me, her face showing the signs of fatigue I have seen perhaps hundreds of times throughout my life—often, when she was home with my brother and me as kids.

"This is farther than I thought," she says, and I feel guilty for schlepping my mother out here in these conditions, wearying her yet again, adding to the total tally across my lifetime. I think of Brad, currently watching sports in my parents' air-conditioned living room, and wonder if he has been the wiser member of this partnership.

But even as we sweat and plod along, there's a real sense of determination in my mother. She often reminds me of something my Nana said: "We have strong women in our family." I see that strength in my mom now—her persistence, good humor, and willingness to be up for a challenge. She has lived many stories on this landscape, many I will never know.

We share a short laugh at the absurdity of our decision—weary, breathless laughs. Dozens of others are walking with us, some stopping occasionally to rest on a bale of hay before going on. In the distance, along a prairie ridge, the horse-drawn wagons we have forsaken carry small crews of people to the site and remind us that we could be working less hard for our symphony experience.

A rider on horseback is positioned at a checkpoint along our path.

"You're doing great. Just a little way to go!" he encourages.

We nod our gratitude between heavy breaths.

During our stay at Clover Cliff Ranch for our anniversary, Brad and I were only a short drive away from the Tallgrass Prairie National Preserve, a piece of the largest remaining tallgrass prairie in the world. Less than four percent of the tallgrass prairie remains, making it one of the most endangered ecosystems on the planet.

One evening, we walked the preserve along another narrow gravel path. The tallgrass prairie is an incredibly diverse and vibrant ecosystem, with hundreds of varieties of grasses, wildflowers, prairie birds, and insects. Since 2009, the preserve has also been dedicated to protecting the largest, most well-known and endangered prairie species—bison. On one section of the path, visitors can pass right by the mighty bison, roaming freely as they once did.

The loss of the bison on the plains is a tragic story, caused by overhunting and even systemic killing by white settlers in the nineteenth century, resulting in their sharp decline and near extinction. During our stay at the ranch, Brad picked up a book in our cabin about the founding of Kansas, and together we lamented that era of our state's history—the way Indigenous people were forced off their homelands, the beauty of the landscape and its creatures slowly eroded and transformed in the name of progress. Kansas is our home—the place where we were both born and raised—but we are not truly native here, the tension of all non-Indigenous Americans.

Alongside our conversations about history, Brad and I also wondered together about the future. For several years, we had been curious whether a move might be ahead for our family. The question was the apex of a much longer conversation, one we had returned to over the years as we made our way through our young parenting days. Specifically, we wondered if it might be time to move back to central Kansas, several hours closer to home, but the time hadn't felt quite right.

But during that stay in the Flint Hills, I felt the weather shift, ever so slightly. Beneath the Kansas sky, our perspective widened. We didn't know what was next for us—would we move back home, or maybe somewhere we hadn't considered?—but we opened up to possibilities, even ones we couldn't imagine.

We walked the nature preserve as dusk began drawing the sun inside its fingers. We paused several times to wait for bison that had moved closer to the trail, but the animals largely ignored us, dropping their massive heads toward the freshly sprouted grass, creamy and vibrant following the Spring's controlled burns. As evening wore on, clouds began moving into the area, shadowing us with their gray undersides. The clouds were so close and present that I felt I could reach up and scrape them. The cloud cover grew thicker as we walked, sheltering most of the day's waning light, but streaks of sunlight poked through and sent crepuscular rays behind the silhouettes of grazing bison, quietly enchanting the whole scene.

Ahead of us, the empty gravel path ran like a train toward the cloudy sky, disappearing over the horizon.

After thirty minutes of walking toward the symphony, my mom and I finally arrive at the concert site, our once cute outfits fully drenched with sweat. There, we find a bustling little prairie town: tents serving barbecue, guides offering prairie walks, a juried art exhibition, and clusters of people sitting on hay bales, listening to experts share about the tallgrass prairie.

We join thousands of others on the grassy incline descending to the stage, finally resting our legs and setting up our chairs. Other attendees spread out their blankets in what resemble tiny crop squares, chatting and sitting in the sun. We take turns getting food and wait for the concert to begin by talking and sitting in the field with a view of the horizon, the hills and limestone outcrops making a curving line against the sky.

Above us, clouds slowly grow in size. The change is nearly imperceptible, but in the hours leading up to the concert, they gradually grow from small, indiscernible puffs into slightly larger cumulus clouds, then faintly graying stratocumulus clouds. I know this from the many photos we take that day, each of us swapping who stands in front of the earth-and-sky backdrop with a cheesy, sunhat-topped smile.

My mom also secretly captures another photo of me that day, in which I am not looking at the camera. Instead, I am looking out into the distance from beneath my floppy hat, toward the Kansas prairie, staring at the line of the horizon I have loved since I was young. My legs are slightly bent, and I am leaning forward, as if I am ready to follow it.

By the time the show starts, our heart rates have returned to normal, and we are newly comfortable with our sweaty selves. As the sun begins to lower in the sky and the temperature cools ever-so-slightly, the symphony begins.

The event is majestic. Gathered in a field with thousands of others, away from any traffic or street noise or climate-controlled buildings, we listen to a full, professional orchestra send its music across the prairie. I will someday fail to remember the title of the pieces played, along with the composers and the movements, but what matters is that we are there, present to the experience, lost in our enjoyment of the music and landscape. We lose track of the weather apps on our phones, our sense of time, our worries about tomorrow, our questions about whether the people sitting around us share our perspectives. We are united in listening to woodwinds, strings, timpani, and the musicians with their years of training and expertise as they make melodic, communal art.

For the first half of that concert, it feels wonderful to be lost in that field—to lose our sense of time and worry. Because as we listen to the performance, there are some things we don't know. Things that will become evident soon, and will surprise us, yet again changing our plans.

In his memoir *Four Seasons in Rome*, Anthony Doerr writes that this state of not knowing is vitally important to human existence: "Not-knowing is always more thrilling than knowing. Not-knowing is where hope and art and possibility and invention come from." I confess I have often held an opposite opinion, believing that not-knowing is daunting, a reminder of my lack of control. And yet, even being here at the symphony now is a result of my not-knowing: not knowing I would be offered tickets, not knowing my mom would come along, not knowing exactly how far we would need to journey to hear the concert, or how lovely the music would be.

Perhaps it's better that we don't know some things, daunting though it may be. Better that we accept what the prairie weather teaches us, according to Kathleen Norris in *Dakota*, when she writes that this region forces us to accept and acknowledge our limits and find ways to live within them.

Indeed, beyond our awareness, the Kansas weather is already doing what it does best—practicing its "significant variability." We don't yet know that at intermission, the members of the symphony will stand and leave the stage, and we will wonder if they are going to take a break, or if there is a reason they might be loading into vans. We don't know that a few minutes later, a man will get on the microphone to make an announcement. The sky will still look calm enough then, but we will learn that a large storm has positioned itself right toward this field, where seven thousand people are sitting without shelter or easy access back to the parking lot.

But soon, we know all of this. At intermission, the show ends.

We had hoped to take the wagons back on our return, especially knowing what we know now, but instead, we turn toward that long path to the parking lot. The wagons are only available for those who truly cannot make the walk, so we begin walking again, this time with seven thousand other people, all of us journeying back to the parking lot together before the storm hits.

For the next hour, we must be a sight to behold—a long line of colorfully dressed humans with hats and chairs, traipsing in a meandering train through the hills. Clouds are now building, spreading more thickly overhead. Tiny nodules poke down from their bellies, a sign severe weather is surely approaching.

My mom walks faster on this return trip, continually glancing up at the sky. She has lived in Kansas for more than six decades and knows how fast a storm can come up or catch you unaware if you aren't paying attention. It's not only that we need to get back to the parking lot, but we still need to drive home.

Although it feels like we are in the middle of a giant herd, we somehow slide out on the front end of the evacuation, making it to our car and out of the parking lot ahead of the incoming rain, hail, and high winds that will eventually cause damage to the tents and other property on site.

As we drive narrow roads leading through the hills, now-billowing storm clouds move across the sky in a low shelf. Through an opening in the clouds from across the prairie, the sun sends its final rays upward, creating a fiery pillar of light just above the horizon.

We slowly make our way back to my parents' house, the same home in which I was raised, again traversing this Kansas landscape full of paradox and contradiction—the ominous lines of a thundercloud crossing the setting sun, beautiful music in a field interrupted by a violent storm, the terrible beauty of the Kantian sublime. This is a landscape that brings ice and snow, rain and tornadoes, wildflower blooms and sweltering heat, sometimes within the same week. The land grieves even as it welcomes, holding both pain and hope. It is the fatigue and determination of my mother, the place where I learned to read the sky and write words, where I have battled elements, pulled over, broken down, suffered and lost and loved and gained. It has been a place to begin and call home, and also a place to continually leave and launch and return.

There are more things my mom and I don't know as we make that drive back. Things that are equal parts exciting and overwhelming, and that will lead us into new layers of joy and grief, but also begin a new adventure. We don't know that in a few short weeks, Brad will get word of a new job, far from the Midwest. And my mom doesn't know that in less than two months, she will get a call from me—again while cruising through the Flint Hills after a reunion with Brad's family—announcing that the job is in Germany, and it looks like instead of moving closer to home, we'll be moving abroad.

Right now, we don't know any of that. We are lost in the not-knowing, that daunting yet thrilling place where many things are possible. We drive across the central Kansas landscape together—me in the passenger seat, my mom leading the way with her knowledge of the region, carefully plotting the best path home by turning down back roads, helping us circumvent the worst of the unpredictable weather.

As we leave the low hills and reenter flat stretches of land, the clouds fully cover our view of the horizon. But we keep driving, staying just ahead of the storm until we arrive safely home, together.

Afterword

My Nana dies in late May, in the quiet of a central Kansas morning, just before sunrise. She has been in a hospice bed for months in the corner of a tiny country home, living out her final days near Valley Center, the same small town where she spent much of her adult life.

Eighteen months ago, she had been there before we boarded our plane for Germany, quietly sitting in her wheelchair atop a swirling gray and purple carpet. She listened and smiled as a small crew of family gathered inside a hotel lobby to send us off, mustering a simple "love you" as we hugged her goodbye.

I knew, then, that she might not be living upon my return to the states. When you move far away, you cognitively understand these things. Still, understanding is one thing and living it out is another, and in the weeks leading up to my Nana's death, I had been futilely searching expensive last-minute plane tickets to Kansas while receiving text updates from my mom, hoping she would live a few weeks longer so I could see her once more when we came home for a scheduled visit. I carried around a low-grade oldest daughter guilt of living across the world while my mother was caring for her own mom in her final days. Distance or not, knowing someone you love is leaving is arduous, a process no one can navigate perfectly.

As one way to keep my Nana company in her final days, my mom began reading to her. I sent some of these essays along in their early versions, as a gesture of connection and to help my mom pass the hours. At the time, I was toiling over whether I would finish these stories, since I was swept up in a new overseas adventure—navigating a new landscape and scenery—unsure how I would ever return to my stories about Kansas when the landscape felt so far away. Besides, as I often thought, I don't even know who these stories are for.

But when my mom read them aloud in the corner of that little farmhouse, she reported that Nana kept her eyes open, paying attention the whole time. When she finished, Nana said in a lilting, raspy voice—what little voice she had left—"keep writing."

I was reminded of Blanche Schwilling, a woman featured in William Least Heat-Moon's *PrairyErth* who lives in Bazaar, Kansas—a town in the Flint Hills that is shrinking, its population down to twelve at the time of Heat-Moon's writing. It no longer has its own postcode or school. But Blanche Schwilling, who served as postmaster for twenty-eight years, has rallied to keep the Methodist church alive. As Heat-Moon writes, "Every Sabbath she rings the bell, but, she says, *Nobody hears it except those of us already there, but I guess that's who it's for.*"

Through my dying grandmother's words across the ocean, I felt invited to keep ringing the bell.

A friend recently reminded me that at the end of *A River Runs Through It*, Norman Maclean writes, "I am haunted by waters." Perhaps, my friend suggested, I am haunted by Kansas.

She may be right. Faith Hill once wrote in *The Atlantic* that our childhood homes always "haunt" us, whether or not our experiences there were positive. After all, our past settings help us make meaning in the present. I began writing these essays during the early days of the pandemic, tucked into my Kansas City home, and I have slowly added to them while riding trains along the Rhine River or sitting at my third-floor desk in Germany. Even as I have embraced and enjoyed new places, these Kansas stories have asked to be attended to. The experience has seemed paradoxical at times, yet Kansas always seems to invite my returning across seasons and times, continuing to inform my own journey of passing through.

On the day my Nana dies, but before I am aware of the news, I am in the passenger seat of a bright blue Toyota as Brad drives us through a rural area in the southeast corner of Belgium. The kids, now eight and ten, are watching shows in the back seat. In a season of significant change and travel, a parent can stand only so many complaints in the car. Brad is listening to a podcast, but as when I was younger, I am staring out the window, trying not to get carsick as we wind through narrow roads and small villages. As we roll through green countryside and past clusters of bakeries, half-timbered houses, and shops, I attempt to revive my rusty college French by reading signs out loud:

Boulangerie

Croix-Rouge

Chez Martine

On our way to a zoo, we cross a large section of open fields beneath a sheet of low-hanging clouds. For a moment, it seems we might be headed the wrong direction, with nothing resembling a zoo or parking lot in sight. The Belgian sky is not quite the Kansas sky, but driving through those empty fields, waiting for our destination to appear on the horizon, I feel somehow at home.

Later, as we are meandering through the exhibits at the zoo, my mom sends a text: Nana is gone from this earthly life. She passed peacefully in the early morning, central time. After I share the news with my family and hug my kids, I lift my phone to make a call back to Kansas. While the phone rings for my mother, I hover outside an exhibit where penguins are waddling their black and white bodies through an enclosure of faux rocks. Nearby, school children laugh and shout to each other in French, and I briefly reflect on my past several hours, wondering where I was while my Nana passed through the end of her life, according to the time in my mom's message.

The recognition meets me with surprising clarity: as when I was younger, traveling to Washington, DC, with Nana encouraging me to look out the window, I was on the road.

Only, this time, years and miles away, no one has to tell me to pay attention.

I already am.

Acknowledgments

One night, during the process of publishing this book, I walked the Tallgrass Prairie with a friend. The sun had already slipped beneath the horizon when we arrived, and before long, we could hardly see the path beneath our feet. But in the darkness, hundreds of fireflies began glittering across the prairie. I was reminded of many moments on my writing journey when the path has seemed equally murky or uncertain, yet the way has been quietly illuminated. Many people have offered friendship, advice, or encouragement, and I regret I cannot name them all here. But special thanks to:

Exhale Creativity, for offering workshops where I wrote and workshopped many early drafts. Ashlee, for creating a safe home for my words and for believing in the goodness of motherhood and art. Callie, for endless encouragement and excellent edits! Sonya, for invaluable feedback on an early sample. Adrienne, I will never forget those two Zoom calls where you looked me in the eye and assured me this project had a future. Thank you for seeing that before I could.

Jen, when I reached out for wisdom about book writing, I could not have predicted that publishing my first book was just over the horizon. Thank you for teaching me about working within my limits and for answering many Voxer messages.

Tracy, Lindsey, and the Meadowlark Team, for welcoming this project and helping me get it into the world. Thank you also for assuring me that I am a Kansan, no matter where in the world I live.

Warren at Eighth Day Books, for the seed of advice that led me to submit to Meadowlark Press. With only a few words, you sent me in the right direction.

Joy, Erin, Emily, JT, Jamie, and Mom, for encouragement and prayers during those final weeks of finishing the manuscript. Kelli, for thoughtful edits and timely words, and Kim, for always believing. Megan, thank you for your calming voice memos and advice about publishing.

The Squirrels (Kelly, Sandee, and Gregory), for reminding me about the joy of art and beauty, and for supplying me with ample doses of haiku and lemon cake.

The Volland Foundation in Alma, Kansas, for creating a lovely gallery space where I wrote the Afterword to this project, long before I knew it would come into the world. And because the book was completed in Germany, thank you also to Living Bakery, Café Wunderbar, and even the Deutsche Bahn for providing both space and time as I finished.

Rick, for many conversations that led me back to writing, and for always reminding me Love is my truest source and deepest home.

My family, for loving me, allowing me to share these stories, and offering both fact corrections and support.

And to Brad and my kids: wherever we live in the world, you make it a home. I love you.

About the Author

Jenna Brack grew up in central Kansas and lived in the Midwest for more than thirty-five years before moving abroad. Her essays and poetry have been featured in publications such as *Every Day Poems*, *The Sunlight Press*, *Coffee + Crumbs*, *105 Meadowlark Reader*, and others. A former educator and college instructor, Jenna now encourages other writers through editing and coaching. She holds an MA in English from Kansas State University and enjoys exploring the goodness of every place alongside her husband and two children. *Pass-Through Place* is her first book.

Notes

A small scene from "The Seat Next to Grandpa" first appeared, in an altered format, in *Fathom Mag*, 2019.

The essay "Dad's Kansas Tours" was first published in *105 Meadowlark Reader: A Kansas Journal of Creative Nonfiction*. Issue #6: Landmarks, November 2023.

Pass-Through Place: An Introduction

Page 4 "a sort of 'spiritual geography' ": Kathleen Norris, *Dakota: A Spiritual Geography* (Mariner, 2001), 2.

The Land Grieves

Page 7 "become the state's namesake": Crystal Douglas, "The Kanza: People of the South Wind" in *Symphony in the Flint Hills Field Journal* (2014): 79, https://newprairiepress.org/sfh/2014/people/3/.

Planted

Page 9 "Mine was a Midwest home": William Stafford, excerpt from "One Home" from *Ask Me: 100 Essential Poems*. Copyright 1954, © 1993, 2014 by William Stafford and the Estate of William Stafford. Reprinted with the permission of The Permissions Company, LLC on behalf of Graywolf Press, Minneapolis, Minnesota, graywolfpress.org.

Page 12 " 'Micropolitan,' several sources say": "Am I Rural?" *Rural Health Information Hub*, accessed March 2025, https://www.ruralhealthinfo.org/am-i-rural#/.

Page 14 "The whole planet is ours": Christie Purifoy, *Roots and Sky: A Journey Home in Four Seasons* (Revell, 2016), 27.

Space, in Four Parts

Page 15 "Dreams take up": William Least Heat-Moon, *Blue Highways: A Journey into America* (Back Bay Books, 2013), 22.

The Seat Next to Grandpa

Page 21 "The time of harvest": *Astonishments: Selected Poems of Anna Kamieńska*, edited and translated by Grazyna Drabik and David Curzon. Translation and compilation copyright 2007 by Grazyna

Drabik and David Curzon. Used by permission of Paraclete Press, www.paracletepress.com.

Dad's Kansas Tours

Page 29 "Almost everything turns out to be interesting": John Green, *The Anthropocene Reviewed: Essays on a Human-Centered Planet* (Dutton, 2021), 276.

Broken Curb

Page 33 "I needed a story": Callie Feyen, *Twirl: My Life with Stories, Writing & Clothes* (T. S. Poetry Press, 2019), 147.

Page 37 "I played a song called 'The Juggler' ": John Thompson, *Teaching Little Fingers to Play* (The Willis Music Company, 1936), 38.

I Told You So

Page 41 "Everyone is a bit scared": Charlie Mackesy, *The Boy, the Mole, the Fox and the Horse* (HarperOne, 2019), 53.

Page 47 "listed as the worst ice storm ever": "Five Worst Kansas Ice Storms," *National Weather Service*, accessed 13 March 2025, https://www.weather.gov/ict/ks_worse_ice_storms.

Tornado Clean-Up

Page 49 "You couldn't get blown around": Leif Enger, *Peace Like a River* (Grove Press, 2001), 56.

Page 51 "The Hero's Journey": Joseph Campbell, *The Hero with a Thousand Faces*, 3rd ed. (New World Library, 2008). Original edition 1949, Bollingen Foundation.

Page 52 "like a person yawned": Ian Frazier, *Great Plains* (Picador, 2001), 15.

Page 55 "I was treated so *gently*": Enger, *Peace Like A River,* 56.

Passing with Care

Page 59 "The best I can ask for": Madeleine L'Engle, *The Irrational Season* (HarperCollins, 1984), 55.

The Red Tree

Page 67 "To open ourselves to love": Stephanie Duncan Smith, *Even After Everything: The Spiritual Practice of Knowing the Risks and Loving Anyway* (Convergent, 2024), 3.

How to See the Sky from the City

Page 73 "Feel the sky": *The Generosity: Poems* by Luci Shaw. Copyright 2020 by Luci Shaw. Used by permission of Paraclete Press, www.paracletepress.com.

Page 76 "in front of Monet's *Water Lilies*": Panel of The Agapanthus Triptych by Claude Monet, The Nelson-Atkins Museum of Art in Kansas City, Missouri.

The Cottonwood Standing by the Highway

Page 77 "The writer operates": Flannery O'Connor, "The Regional Writer" in *Mystery and Manners: Occasional Prose*, eds. Sally and Robert Fitzgerald (Farrar, Straus and Giroux, 1969), 59.

Page 80 "The LORD is my shepherd": Robert Alter, *The Book of Psalms: A Translation with Commentary* (Norton, 2009), 148, Kindle.

Page 81 "I played when I lost them": Mary Victoria Huston, *My Pomes.* ed. Ted Huston (pub. by editor, 1995), 7.

Page 81 "the old one's shape": Huston, *My Pomes*, 7.

Page 82 "the way Naomi Shihab Nye describes": Naomi Shihab Nye, "Famous" from *Words Under the Words: Selected Poems* (Eighth Mountain, 1994).

Farm Road

Page 85 "Every place": Anthony Doerr, *Four Seasons in Rome: On Twins, Insomnia and the Biggest Funeral in the History of the World* (4th Estate, 2008), 186.

Page 87 "much like Madeleine L'Engle describes": Madeleine L'Engle, *A Circle of Quiet* (HarperCollins), 4.

Page 89 "I would never have thought": Marilynne Robinson, *Gilead* (Farrar, Straus, and Giroux, 2004), 15.

Bats and Bees (and Mice and Wasps)

Page 91 "Like Jacob's angel": Norris, *Dakota*, 1.

Keys from My Grandma

Page 95 "Whatever we have been given": Lewis Hyde, *The Gift: Creativity and the Artist in the Modern World* (Vintage Books, 2007), 4.

Scenic Overlook

Page 101 "I asked what was so special": William Least Heat-Moon, *PrairyErth:A Deep Map* (Houghton Mifflin, 1991), 193.

Page 104 "Like a replicating virus": Green, *The Anthropocene Reviewed*, 253.

Page 105 "precisely because it isn't easy": Green, *The Anthropocene Reviewed*, 218.

Page 105 "there's no place like home": *The Wizard of Oz*, directed by Victor Fleming, MGM, 1939.

Mile Markers

Page 107 "As they pass through": Psalm 84:6. Scripture taken from the New King James Version®. Copyright © 1982 by Thomas Nelson. Used by permission. All rights reserved.

Page 109 "open space in all directions": Kosuke Koyama, *Three Mile an Hour God* (SCM Press, 1979), 4.

Page 110 "In the words of Louisiana Elefante's teacher": Kate DiCamillo, *Louisiana's Way Home* (Candlewick, 2018), 114.

Leaving at Intermission

Page 113 "the place our mothers and fathers": Wyatt Townley, "Centering the House" in *The Afterlives of Trees* (Woodley Press, 2011), 31. Used with permission from the author.

Page 115 "Will the weather": Dave Kendall, "Symphony in the Flint Hills Taps into the Restorative Power of the Kansas Prairie," *Kansas Reflector*, June 7, 2022, kansasreflector.com/2022/06/07/symphony-in-the-flint-hills-taps-into-restorative-power-of-the-kansas-prairie/.

Page 115 "At its heart": Kendall, *Reflector.*

Page 117 "significant variability": "Kansas Weather and Climate," *Travel Kansas*, accessed February 15, 2025, https://www.travelks.com/plan-your-trip/travel-info/weather-and-climate/

Page 117 "merely players": William Shakespeare, *As You Like It* (Penguin Books, 2000), act 2, scene 7, line 140.

Page 118 "less than four percent": "Tallgrass Prairie," *National Preserve Kansas*, accessed February 15, 2025, https://www.nps.gov/tapr/learn/nature/a-complex-prairie-ecosystem.htm.

Page 121 "Not-knowing is always more thrilling": Doerr, *Four Seasons in Rome,* 154.

Page 121 "Better that we accept": Norris, *Dakota*, 120.

Afterword

Page 126 "Every Sabbath": Heat-Moon, *PrairyErth,* 182.

Page 126 "I am haunted": Norman Maclean, *A River Runs Through It and Other Stories* (University of Chicago, 2017), page 118, Kindle.

Page 126 "Faith Hill once wrote": Faith Hill, "Your Childhood Home Might Never Stop Haunting You," in *The Atlantic*, 17 May 2024.

Bibliography

Alter, Robert. *The Book of Psalms: A Translation with Commentary.* Norton, 2009, Kindle.

Campbell, Joseph. *The Hero with a Thousand Faces: The Collected Works of Joseph Campbell,* 3rd ed. New World Library, 2008.

DiCamillo, Kate. *Louisiana's Way Home.* Candlewick, 2018.

Doerr, Anthony. *Four Seasons in Rome: On Twins, Insomnia and the Biggest Funeral in the History of the World.* 4th Estate, 2008.

Douglas, Crystal. "The Kanza: People of the South Wind." *Symphony in the Flint Hills Field Journal* (2014):78-81, https://newprairiepress.org/sfh/2014/people/3.

Enger, Leif. *Peace Like a River.* Grove Press, 2001.

Feyen, Callie. *Twirl: My Life with Stories, Writing & Clothes.* T. S. Poetry Press, 2019.

Frazier, Ian. *Great Plains.* Picador, 2001.

Green, John. *The Anthropocene Reviewed: Essays on a Human-Centered Planet.* Dutton, 2021.

Hill, Faith. "Your Childhood Home Might Never Stop Haunting You." *The Atlantic,* 17 May 2024. https://www.theatlantic.com/family/archive/2024/05/childhood-home-memory-identity/678399/.

Heat-Moon, William Least. *Blue Highways: A Journey into America.* Back Bay Books, 2013.

Heat-Moon, William Least. *PrairyErth: A Deep Map.* Houghton Mifflin, 1991.

Huston, Mary Victoria. *My Pomes.* Edited by Ted Huston. Published by editor, 1995.

Hyde, Lewis. *The Gift: Creativity and the Artist in the Modern World.* Vintage Books, 2007.

Kamieńska, Anna. "The Time of Harvest and the Time of Poems is Passing." In *Astonishments: Selected Poems of Anna Kamieńska*. Edited by Grażyna Drabik and David Curzon. Paraclete Press, 2007.

Kendall, Dave. "Symphony in the Flint Hills Taps into the Restorative Power of the Kansas Prairie." *Kansas Reflector*, June 7, 2022. https://kansasreflector.com/2022/06/07/symphony-in-the-flint-hills-taps-into-restorative-power-of-the-kansas-prairie/.

Koyama, Kosuke. *Three Mile An Hour God.* SCM Press, 1979.

L'Engle, Madeleine. *A Circle of Quiet.* HarperCollins, 1984.

L'Engle, Madeleine. *The Irrational Season.* HarperCollins, 1984.

Mackesy, Charlie. *The Boy, the Mole, the Fox and the Horse.* HarperOne, 2019.

Maclean, Norman. *A River Runs Through It and Other Stories.* University of Chicago, 2017. Kindle.

National Preserve Kansas. "Tallgrass Prairie." Accessed February 15, 2025. https://www.nps.gov/tapr/learn/nature/a-complex-prairie-ecosystem.htm.

National Weather Service. "Five Worst Kansas Ice Storms." Accessed 13 March 2025. https://www.weather.gov/ict/ks_worse_ice_storms.

Norris, Kathleen. *Dakota: A Spiritual Geography.* Mariner, 2001.

Nye, Naomi Shihab. *Words Under the Words: Selected Poems.* Eighth Mountain Press, 1994.

O'Connor, Flannery. *Mystery and Manners: Occasional Prose.* Edited by Sally and Robert Fitzgerald. Farrar, Straus, and Giroux, 1969.

Purifoy, Christie. *Roots and Sky: A Journey Home in Four Seasons.* Revell, 2016.

Robinson, Marilynne. *Gilead.* Farrar, Straus, and Giroux, 2004.

Rural Health Information Hub. "Am I Rural?" Accessed March 2025. ruralhealthinfo.org.

Shakespeare, William. *As You Like It.* Penguin Books, 2001.

Shaw, Luci. *The Generosity: Poems.* Paraclete Press, 2020.

Smith, Stephanie Duncan. *Even After Everything: The Spiritual Practice of Knowing the Risks and Loving Anyway.* Convergent, 2024.

Spufford, Francis. *Light Perpetual.* Scribner, 2021.

Stafford, William. *Ask Me: 100 Essential Poems.* Graywolf Press, 2014.

Townley, Wyatt. *The Afterlives of Trees.* Woodley Press, 2011.

Travel Kansas. "Kansas Weather and Climate." Accessed February 15, 2025. https://www.travelks.com/plan-your-trip/travel-info/weather-and-climate/.

Books are a way to explore, connect, and discover. Reading gives us the gift of living lives and gaining experiences beyond our own.

Publishing books is our way of saying:
we love these words,
we want to preserve them,
we want to play a role in sharing them with the world.

MEADOWLARKBOOKSTORE.COM

Follow Meadowlark Press
on Facebook & Instagram

facebook.com/ReadAMeadowlarkBook

@meadowlarkbooks

Memoirs from Meadowlark Press

And I Cried, Too: Confronting Evil in a Small Town
Mike Hartnett

The Big Quiet: One Woman's Horseback Ride Home
Lisa D. Stewart

A Cow for College and Other Stories of 1950s Farm Life
James Kenyon

Gravedigger's Daughter: Vignettes from a Small Kansas Town
Cheryl Unruh

Headwinds
Edna Bell-Pearson

Jigsaw Puzzling: Essays in a Time of Pestilence
Denise Low

www.ingramcontent.com/pod-product-compliance
Lightning Source LLC
Chambersburg PA
CBHW031334060726
47590CB00007B/2468
* 9 7 8 1 9 5 6 5 7 8 9 1 1 *